The South African Cross

THE
SOUTH
AFRICAN
Cross

Joe Odiboh

(Winner: African Leadership
and Excellence Award, 2012, Ireland)

Published by: Editions Dedicaces LLC
  12759 NE Whitaker Way, Suite D833
  Portland, Oregon, 97230
  www.dedicaces.us

Library of Congress Cataloging-in-Publication Data
  Odiboh, Joe.
  The South African Cross / by Joe Odiboh.
  p. cm.

  ISBN-13: 978-1-77076-506-1 (alk. paper)
  ISBN-10: 1-77076-506-9 (alk. paper)

About the Author

Mr. Joe Odiboh is a South African citizen by naturalization, and he is originally from Nigeria. Born on the 9th Day of May, 1960, he is an art teacher, contemporary artist, actor, Security Service Provider, Comedian, Writer and a Master of Ceremonies.

He went to Namibia, and later to South Africa from Nigeria in 1994 where he acquired the South African citizenship by naturalization.

While in Ireland in 2011, he found himself under prevailing circumstances at that time, and rediscovered his hopes and dreams, which made him win the "African Leadership and Excellence Award" 2012, in arts and culture, sponsored by the African Voice Newspapers in Ireland. He is an African artist who has donated some of his paintings to the Irish government, Sligo County Borough, Sligo General Hospital, Bridgestock, Citi Link Network International, Dublin, a branch of Citi Bank, and other organizations, institutions, and individuals. He is the Chairman of Globe House Residents Union in Sligo, Ireland and author of yet to be published book, "Critical Assignment" featuring (The South African Cross). He has done several volunteer art workshops and took part in art exhibitions in Sligo, Dublin and in Poland. He took part in The Sabona Community movie Productions by Loch Bo Films, and Sligo Films production, "The Encounter", and he is the lead actor of the short Irish film, "Fuaite Faite". He is now a contemporary artist with numerous paintings and has gained recognitions with Peace 111 New Urban Peace Collective sponsored by the EU.

He is a member of Sabona Group for Sligo Peace Capacity Building Project funded by Peace 111 Programme, through the European Union's Regional Development Fund.

Dedication

Dedicated to late former President Nelson Mandela of South Africa, and in recognition of the United States first black President Barrack Obama, both of them representing the symbol of hopes and dreams for all mankind.

<u>To Late former President Nelson Mandela with love</u>

Between November 1994 and February 1995, former President Nelson Mandela visited me nearly every day in my dreams at Surrey Estate, Athlone, Cape Town, in South Africa.

During his visits, we both discussed various issues and problems in South Africa and world affairs as it affects the people and humanity and sought ways to remedy the situation. He was so impressed with my contributions and friendship that he nominated me his special Political Adviser in his cabinet.

The ANC was divided over my appointment as a foreign immigrant from Nigeria. After series of deliberations in various dreams, the parliament hesitantly ratified my appointment and I continued in my service as Adviser to the former President Nelson Mandela in my vain dreams.

On the 18th Day of July 1996, as an act of fate, my daughter was born on the same birthday with former President Nelson Mandela at the Mowbray Maternity Hospital, in Cape Town. That same night, the former President Nelson Mandela visited me to wish my daughter very good tidings and celebrate with me in my dreams.

We both joked and laughed like school kids about life and what the future holds for the people of South Africa. He was very cheerful and charismatic, the best friend and father I ever had in my vain dreams. On a very serious note, he looked at me intently and urged me to write a book based on all the issues and problems as discussed during all his visits. He asked me to write these things exactly the way they are without fear or favour, and to help seek ways to remedy the situation. We looked at each other for a while, smiled, and said in unison, "The Mandela Legacies".

It was like a big joke. He got up and we shook hands, and I thought to myself silently and quietly, "Ctitical Assignment". He smiled at me strangely with confidence and went his own way, never to visit me again in my dreams to this day. Though it was all unrealistic dreams, I did not treat this issue as one, believing there is a reason and purpose for these dreams.

In December 1994, I made a painting of Mandela carrying the child of former Communications Minister under his regime, Jay Naidoo, and went to Cape Argus Newspapers with hope of assisting me in presenting the painting to former President Nelson Mandela. After taking my pictures with the painting for publication in the newspapers by Cape Argus photographer, they asked for my personal information and details in regards my profile. Realizing that I was an undocumented illegal immigrant, I took my painting and went undercover for my own safety and security. I later donated the painting to the Red Cross in 1996.

That same year on June 4th 1996, I became the first Nigerian immigrant to be granted Permanent residence status and also the first person to be granted citizenship in 1998. I wrote a premature manuscript, entitled "The Mandela Comedy" and sought for help to publish this book with the help of all important personalities and South African Parliament and executives, as well as publishers and the presidency. Help was hard to find.

I then contacted Nelson Mandela and the Nelson Mandela Foundation responded that the name of Nelson Mandela was exclusively reserved for 'Nelson Mandela Children's Fund'. I let go my pipe dream and eventually lost that manuscript. I am glad that I lost that manuscript because of the recent developments in South Africa and in world affairs.

In compliance with the wish of 'Nelson Mandela Foundation', or Nelson Mandela Children Fund, I have decided not to use the name of Nelson Mandela in the title for this book. I have therefore chosen the title: "The South African Cross". I chose this title 24 hours before the news of Mandela's exit. The title came to me as a vision in my dreams in Ireland as a suitable replacement for the other title I chose, "South Africa: Hopes and Dreams".

This title came to me like a revelation of his exit and the former title in concert with the abridged title have shaped the final edition of this book. This present title did not only come to me as an act of fate in his exit, but it has given me a great opportunity to be wise in the way I dealt with the problems in South Africa and world problems. It has afforded me the opportunity to reflect on the problems of other nations and the problems of the world.

While in Ireland in 2011, I have found my lost destiny and rediscovered my hopes and dreams. I have become more exposed to the reality of a better life and a better tomorrow for all mankind. Now that the father of all nations is gone to rest in eternal peace in the lord, I will not be afraid, nor will I waver in my commitment to write a book that will help reshape the destiny of the South African people, and all the peoples of the world. Today, I stand tall and firm in this commitment to better mankind, and knowing that God and his wisdom is on my side in the realization of this dream.

As a fine artist and actor, I have decided to paint the pictures of South Africa problems and solutions in black and white colours which are the neutral colours in life. I have decided to act out as an actor in painting the face of the world, not as a literary artist but as a visual or fine artist, painting and repainting same issues in hope of creating a visual picture of the problems and solutions to all our problems and world crises. I have written this book without fear or favour not as a sycophant but as a seer without bias bearing a cross.

I have confirmed to my humble self that the beginning of wisdom is the ability to call things by their right names. I have tried in my sense of judgement and reasoning to help all South Africans and the world in general to rethink, and have a change of heart and attitude in the part to peace, truth and reconciliation in life, and in ensuring that we can all hope for a better life for all on earth.

I believe this is why God have kept me alive all these years to make this dream come true. I know that I am not an English student but a humanist, and that it is better to write something as an artist than to write nothing as an Englishman. It is better to be a hopeful man in life, than being hopeless in this world of social injustice and escalating acts of terrorism.

If need be that today I die after the publication of this book, I will be glad to join with Madiba in the final place of rest. I will be most relieved to present him with a copy of this book in the world beyond, and rest with him in eternal peace. I will be glad that my life in South Africa and on earth; have not come to waste. I will be glad that I was born a Nigerian from very noble parents, and that in my lifetime, I have tried and done my utmost best to help resolve the problems of injustice, poverty, racial bias, crime and violence, and all those ills and vices in society which tend to create a divide in the common bonds that hold us together as a people.

I am pleased that I have used this opportunity in the Art of Asylum in Ireland to express myself and reflect on other issues relating to Nigeria my fatherland, Africa my continent, and most other nations on earth. I will be glad that the dream of over twenty years ago in my life with late former President Nelson Mandela have been finally realized and fully accomplished.

By Author: Joe Odiboh

Famous Quotes by the Author:

Ideal leadership and the practicality of power requires true and just leadership to live in discomfort, insecurity, pains, unhappiness, and hunger to understand the discomfort, pains, unhappiness, insecurity and hunger of the people who are victims of injustice and terror in society.

Any leadership, which ignores being part of the plights and suffering of the people, and remains at ease while the people are no-longer at ease, is like a garden full of weeds.

Author: Joe Odiboh

Contents

Chapter 1
Hopes and Dreams

When former President Nelson Mandela urged me to write this book in my vain dreams, I realized at once that this was a very critical assignment. Writing about the complex problems, ways and means in South Africa, and reflecting on the problems of the world is not in any way an easy task. It was a critical assignment that must be done.

One thing I know is that once upon a time in South Africa, the world was bereaved with the exit of the greatest legend of our time, former President Nelson Mandela. Following this great loss to humanity, many people wonder about the future of this country long after apartheid is gone and forgotten. People around the world are appreciative of the sacrifices and efforts made by former President Nelson Mandela and many others to bring about freedom, democracy and justice for all in this country.

The long and lasting legacy of goodwill established by late former President Nelson Mandela is the legacy of peace, truth, reconciliation, love, equal rights and justice not only for all South Africans, but also for all mankind. This is the legacy being celebrated by all mankind in the declaration of Mandela Day by the United Nations. It is a recognition of the need for everyone in life to do good at least for an hour a day for a better tomorrow in human cause. This is something we must continue to celebrate in the life of this great legend. The more good we do everyday in our lives the better the society.

We all know that man is a product of mortality and that life is like a market place where everyone comes to trade and go back home at different times after buying or selling. How and when we return back to our creator after fulfilling our missions and purpose on earth is a matter for the merciful or merciless whip of fate, as the case may be, or may not be. We should all play our positive roles in life, but when we buy something, we must pay for it. For the price of treason and crimes against humanity, there is a price; and if you are guilty, you are going to pay the price. All we need is love and a better life for all on earth.

While we appreciate the good works of this great legend, we must as a people learn to appreciate the efforts of the government in South Africa, whether they are perfect or imperfect and become part of that government's efforts to do well for the common good of all South Africans, and use this opportunity to at least try to live exemplary life to change the fortunes of all mankind. This is the first step to self realization and a quest to make South Africa a better place for all to live.

Our ways and means in life must become useful lessons for world leadership, and the leadership in South Africa. One way of honouring our hearts in South Africa is for the people of this country to appreciate the good efforts and hard work of government to educate its people and bring about better life for all. We cannot do this by bringing about negative influences in society, but through unity in diversity, love for one another, patriotism, hard work, discipline, industry and enterprise. This kind of national cause is what is lacking in South Africa today. Despite all the great efforts on the part of the South African government, we still see terrible incidents of rapes and gruesome murders, police brutality, escalating rate of criminality and infidelity, immorality, untold violence, and people who still live in abject poverty.

There is racial bias and lack of patriotism. Everything wrong in society is being unjustly blamed on the South African government. The government cannot be blamed for the evils that men do. The South African government did not shoot and kill their national football soccar goalkeeper. The truth is that celebrating the ideals and good work of Nelson Mandela is one thing, but living according to the ideals and the principles of peace, truth, and reconciliation is another thing entirely. Its' just that most people in South Africa have refused to imbibe the spirit of patriotism, and this lack of love and patriotism in this country is the genesis and real bane of South Africa problems.

While some reasonable and good people in the society and patriots are doing their utmost best to make South Africa a better place to live, there are other elements in society whose aim it is to destabilize the new political order, and drag to the mud the economic and social gains already achieved in this country. These reactionary forces in the society are many and they outweigh the positive forces in society. These evil forces are battling to dampen the good efforts of government. Prominent among these forces of evil, are the forces of crime and violence, as well as the forces of race hate and corruption.

There are many other people who are not happy to witness majority rule and do not wish to see people with mixed colours and other nationals live side by side in a peaceful and coherent thriving society. Most of these people are the forces of racism and xenophobia. Their wish is to live isolated lives devoid of togetherness and love. These are the people who are afraid of competition, and do not wish to see all South Africans and visitors to the land living side by side in harmony.

Others are economic forces and those people who do not wish for the rationalization of the nation's resources, the growth of the new generation, and they are determined in ensuring that those who have been disadvantaged by the apartheid policies of the past do not see the light of hope to new and better beginnings in life. They wish the past to remain in the present. These people are our brothers and sisters of pro-apartheid era and enemies of progress in society.

These are some of the problems the South African government and leadership have to contend with in the hope of making very meaningful difference in the lives of their people. These are very complex problems for the government, and even so, the government is doing its utmost best to create a balance between the good, the bad, and the ugly. How much progress the government have done in this regards or what impact their efforts have been in our lives is something for which we must hold ourselves to blame.

People must learn to have a change of heart, think and act positively in society and take full opportunity of self-empowerment through black affirmative action of government, as well as all good government programs and policies. We must stop to blame the government for everything wrong in our lives. Even when things are not wrong in our lives, some people make the wrong choices and do every wrong thing in society. This is not good for the legacy Mandela left behind for all our children. This is very unhealthy for national growth and development.

We must establish the legacy of helping the government to create everything good in this country and everything right in our lives. We must not forget so easily that the true definition of democracy implies government of the people, by the people, and for the people. This means that what the people are, and what the people want, is what the people do in their private lives and in government. The failure of a government is the failure of the people. This is because the peole must tell the govenment what they want the government to do, and which the leaders must legislate because they represent the people.

As wonderful people of this great nation, let us see the legacies of Nelson Mandela as the lengthened shadows in our acts and deeds in society. We must not allow the negative actions of some people in society, and our individual actions and deeds to bring us sorrow, tears, and blood. What kind of people we are as individuals is what defines the life and destiny of the people of our nation. If we chose to follow the part of righteousness and moral values, we will experience peace, stability and progress in our lives, and in the life of our nation.

Since charity begins at home, our people must begin as a duty and personal moral responsibility to contribute meaningfully to the life of this great nation. This is one way of celebrating the life of Nelson Mandela. We must not forget that the tears in our eyes is the tears Nelson Mandela and others shed for us in the sacrifices they made to let our people experience the promised land. Our tears are covered by the supreme prices most South Africans paid to set us free. Our tears is covered by the blood of all those who died to set us free from bondage.

If we wish to weep for the suffering and pains of Nelson Mandela as he left us, let us weep for ourselves and bemoan our acts and deeds in this great nation. Nelson Mandela and others have already done their utmost best for the good of our generation and future generations to come. It is for us as a people to place upon our heads and shoulders the tasks of doing our utmost best for South Africa in other to reap the gains of posterity. We must now stand strong and firm in the journey Mandela and others have led us.

This is what we can do if people must stop to neglect their moral rights and civic responsibilities. We must take stock of the development and unity of this nation, and stop demonizing our society and leadership.

We must play active political roles and become part of the government, and help encourage and steer the government to a smooth and graded road to true peace and progress in our land. Peace and progress cannot be truly achieved in this country by the expansion and creation of informal settlements and illegal structures by our black and Afrikaans brothers and sisters. We know there are great difficulties in society and abject poverty, but we must not accept this as part of our culture and national heritage. We must strive to expell poverty and illegal structures from our lives. Mandela has not led us to create a kind of place where poverty, hate, crime, racial bias, disruption and violence reign supreme. True peace and progress cannot dominate our national agenda without the help of our people to help the government to help the nation.

In principles of life, people who cannot help themselves cannot help others and cannot help the nation. This is why we need to re-evaluate our hearts and minds and face the truth and reality of life; knowing that only us as individuals, as communities, and as a people can change the course of destiny in this nation. We can do this by being useful to ourselves, to our communities, and to the nation. By being useful to ourselves and society, we become useful to our nation and humanity. It is important to know that the government of any nation is inseparable from its people. We cannot separate the people of South Africa from the government because we are one and the same people. The people own the government, and the government represent the people. We must understand that any negative influence we make as individuals and as communities or race, or in any crime or evil committed in our society; it boomerangs back on us as a people and as government.

If our government is progressive, it is to our credit. On the other hand, if our government is backward, we have ourselves to blame. This is determined by our conducts as individuals and as communities. We must learn to blame ourselves for the state of the nation rather than blame other people or government. We have a moral right and civic responsibility to defend our constitution and our country or national pride, by ensuring that our society and community is a better place for us to live in and prosper in life. This is what Mandela wanted for all South Africans. We must do this through political participation and strict obedience to the national constitution.

Good ways of life enable peace and progress in society, while negatives acts and deeds breed poverty, backwardness, crime and violence. We need to make that choice now, right now in which decision we make for which road we must take. The people in society and in our various communities are human beings in a human race with choices to decide the future of our generations.

We must accept the fact that Nelson Mandela and many others have done their utmost best as human beings to give us freedom and democracy in South Africa. We must also accept the fact that it is so sad to see many communities are still segregated in several settlements on racial line. Many black and coloureds people still live in informal settlements, and in the settlements created for them by the apartheid government of the past.

It is time we all start to live together as one without any particular settlement for any particular race or colour. It is time for white people to relocate to Soweto and black settlements and live among our people as one. It is time to live together as mixed race and colour in all the communities. We must do this with togetherness and love in the way Mandela taught us to do. While Mandela has given us hope to aspire to greater heights in life, we must stop to have people who have lost faith in life and in the new democratic order. These are people who do not appreciate the virtues of hard work and cannot make better use of the black affirmative actions of government.

These are people who have made the wrong choices in life and have resolved to be enemies to their own destiny. These people must have a change of heart and learn from history that there is dignity in labour. The government and the state of the nation cannot make meaningful progress if we as individuals do not make the sacrifices necessary to better our lives and the life of our nation and humanity. This is the principle for a better life and a better tomorrow for all mankind. This principle require us to try and become better people on earth through our own acts and deeds in society.

We do not need to become the type of people who do not know the difference between progress and backwardness simply because we have never aspired to greater heights in life. It is a good thing to try doing something progressive and meaningful in life, and know the meaning of hard work, toil, and anxious moments. We must learn how to sow seeds and wait for them to grow, nourish and water them, and protect them in other to reap its rewards. We must try to know what it is to have foresight, patience in working and waiting, and decline any interest in negative impact on society. The future is not a thing of the past.

Let us not become the kind of people who have ignored and refused to celebrate freedom and democracy. We must remain positive as Mandela and others did in prison by exploring life to its fullest potentials through hard work, dedication, and ideal citizenship. Let us follow the good examples of Europe and the civilized world. Everyone needs to know their civic responsibilities and obligations to the nation. We know that life is difficult and not perfect in the civilized world, but it is still far better than those in the so called third world countries because we have made it so. Becoming a first world or third world country is a matter of the choices we make in life. While the people in the third world countries are still crying and moaning for a better life and a glorious world order, we in the third or seventh world countries are mourning our fate not knowing we are the captains of our ship and masters of our fate.

The issue of the third or fourth world countries inside one earth which God gave to us all will never arise if the people in these poor nations and their governments make the necessary sacrifices and efforts to be better people. A true and just government must become accountable to their people while our people must become accountable to our various communities and society. This is the checks and balances we need to make a difference in the life of our nation. Being ignorant of this principle of truth and justice for all is not an excuse for backwardness and torpidity in society.

The government in South Africa therefore cannot be said to be perfect, but at least in comparison with other African nations, it can be said that it is doing its best to educate and provide for our people. We know that a lot of people are ready to compliment the efforts of government through proper education, skills development, business, enterprise, sports, and recreation. It is so sad however that many others are derailing the good efforts of government instead of helping the government to help themselves make South Africa a better place to live. This act of cowardice and infidelity is unpatriotic and uncivilized, and we must change our attitude towards life in the positive affirmative.

We know that there are people, especially the black people and some people in the coloured communities who have got gainful employments, and could afford bonds and mortgages to buy their own houses. Many others have been given RDP houses by the government. Many of these gainfully employed people must not squander their incomes and create unhealthy illegal structures in informal settlements where they will not pay rent, water bills and electricity utility bills. There are other people who technically adjust their electricity meters in such a way that it does not read energy usage whereby defrauding the nation of the revenue needed for national growth and development.

Gainful employment is an opportunity to buy and own your own houses and properties. It is important that we say 'No' to living in squalor or illegal structures in informal settlements. We must take responsibility in life to live a better life, purchase and own your house and property. We must take responsibility in the payments of rates and utility bills. That is how good and responsible people must live their lives in dignity and purpose. That is how we must endeavour to live in South Africa as responsible citizens.

We must not use our freedom to spend our incomes unwisely by making the government seem as if it was doing nothing for the black and coloured communities. We must not develop the spirit of erecting more illegal structures and wait till eternity for free RDP houses. Our people must learn that most white people bought their homes, houses and properties on loans and mortgages which they pay off responsibly over a long period of time. This is why most of them live good lives because that is the choice they made in life.

Let us also as black and coloured people follow their good examples and make the necessary sacrifices to move from grass to grace. We must stop the culture of waiting and depending solely on the government to provide us with properties and RDP houses. We can make our lives better in this country if we choose to rise to greater heights in life. There is nobody who is born with a property or house from the mother's womb except through inheritance from sacrifices made by their parents and those before them. Houses are built and created by individuals or home owners from the time of creation. This is something anyone can own if we work and plan towards home or properties ownership.

Nelson Mandela is not the father of illegal structures in illegal settlements; he is the father of peace and progress in our lives. He will be very sad in heaven above to continue to see our people living in squalor or abject poverty in illegal settlements. We must celebrate his life on earth by his hopes and dreams to make South Africa a better place to live. We must use his life as a celebration of the challenges we face in this country. We must feel challenged enough to abandon the reckless life most of us live and search for a better life.

We must continue in our search for the hero inside of us. We must reflect on our lives and our living conditions in life and ask ourselves couples of questions regarding our wants and needs. We must learn to prioritize the basic necessities of life, and what our hopes and dreams are. We must believe that living a responsible and noble life is a task that must be done, and we must work towards achieving our aims and objectives in life. We must shy away from the obnoxious thoughts that taking up the responsibility of owning our own homes and paying for them is an exclusive reserve of only the white people.

This is where proper education is most essential in individual growth and development. Most educated people will not think or behave that way. Sad, as this situation might seem, some people in some highly impoverished areas in the society have formed the culture of social irresponsibility and waste their social welfare money on alcohol and drugs, making life miserable for themselves and their children. People should not behave this way. It is unhealthy and does not help the family and community development.

It is not wise for people to waste their meagre resources for unwholesome acts.

We also know of people who result to spending days in rubbish dumps sites waiting for dirt to arrive by rubbish dump trucks from faraway in more affluent suburbs or cities, so that

they can scramble through the rubbish dumps for something to eat or drink, as if the government do not care for their needs, or simply because they have resigned themselves to hunger and starvation, or abject poverty.

Even if the government cares for their needs, one thing is certain that a lot of people are very poor and impoverished in the Southern African region. There is no one whose needs are met that will wait to feed from rubbish dumps. There is no one on earth that will make a choice between feeding from the dustbin and the dinner table. Unless mad people. Even mad people still prefer to beg for food than to feed from the bin. The issue of poverty in South Africa is a man made problem that must be eradicated in society because South Africa has some of the greatest mechanized farms and farmlands on earth, and a food exporting nation. Any freedom that is not accompanied with a better life for all is no freedom in the real sense of the word. What we don't need in this nation is freedom of poverty.

Here, in some national documentaries on television screens, we see in great sadness faces of families, mother and child, children and babies scrambling through rubbish dumps for contaminated leftovers to eat and contaminated drinks from the bin to drink. These are old men and women, young men and women, and babies who are the future of South Africa.

The good thing is that apartheid is dead and buried a long time ago in South Africa, freedom and democracy is thriving. Even so, our people think that those in positions of authority are seemingly seen as having the best of life like the masters in the book, "Animal Farm", drinking fresh milk. However critical this assertion might be, a better life for all is the key to social equality and true justice. This will help reduce the incidents of crime in society. These critics seem to forget that those in positions of authority are public servants who are working day and night to build for their people and their children a better tomorrow. Our leaders are responsible people who live responsible lives in their respective households. They deserve decent wages and good life in other to be competent in their duties to the people. This does not include corrupt practices.

Our politicians and public servants are showing good examples of how to live good lives so that the masses can follow their good examples. These good examples of ideal leadership will better be followed if the ordinary people also have a taste of the good life being lived by their leaders and public servants. This should reflect in salaries and wages of our workers, and an effective social welfare system to provide for those who are unable to gain meaningful employment, the disabled people, the pensioners and those who are too old to fend for themselves.

Ideal leadership and the practicality of power requires true and just leadership to live in discomfort, insecurity, unhappiness, and hunger to understand the discomfort, pains, unhappiness, insecurity and hunger of the people who are victims of injustice and terror in society. Any leadership, which ignores being part of the plights and suffering of the people, and remains at ease while the people are no-longer at ease, is like a garden full of weeds.

Accountability does not only mean the declaration of assets of public servants, or in whatever ways or means. It simply means that the government must give to the people with the resources of the state a better life for all and all the goodies that truly fulfil the promise of true independence. These include good government policies and service delivery, good social welfare system that ignores poverty and raises the standard of living of ordinary South Africans. Accountability involves the provision of a better life for all South Africans and eradication of poverty from our national life, safety and security of lives and properties.

We do not need to kill and rob other people to be like the politicians and live like our leaders with dignity. Many people believe our leadership is robbing the government treasury through corruption and greed. While the government must try to make the lives of the ordinary South Africans become like those of the politicians, we must learn to work hand in hand with the government to stop the circle of poverty in society. There are too many options open to us through government programs and agendas for self empowerment. We can live better than the politicians and public servants if we take advantage of the good programs and government agendas, and work very hard and sincerely to raise our standard of living.

There is hardly any country on earth where public servants and politicians do not have good living conditions, and South African leaders cannot be exempted from the good things of life which they also seek for the electorates. It is a good thing for public servants to live fruitful lives in other to know and understand what is also good for the ordinary people in society. As leadership live fruitful lives, they too must ensure that those masses that put them in positions of authority remain as fruitful as well. It is no use drinking fresh milk while the ordinary South Africans are drinking sour milk, 'Amanzi' to fill their stomachs. Soured milk, 'Amanzi' cannot be used for tea and coffee which we need daily to calm our nerves and anger.

South African leaders are working day and night, and they are not as greedy and corrupt as what we see of other leaders and public servants in most other African nations, or the rest part of the world. They are very simple people, and humble leaders who are accountable to their people the best way they can. Everyone of them cannot be said to be innocent, but many of them can be said to be innocent. They are far from being like most other African and world leaders who wish to live and die in power, greedy for wealth, and behave like thin gods before those who placed them in positions of authorities.

However, there is nothing like small or big corruption. A corrupt mind corrupts the society. Corruption is corruption, and it remains an endemic ebola virus in society and must never be allowed to happen. The real ebola in society is the curruption and greed in Africa, especially in West Africa. This corruption have become an ebola virus in the animals we eat in West Africa. This is because what goes around comes around. South African leaders must not behave like most other African leaders, because if they do, there will be tears in the eyes of all South Africans. Even so, we know that South Africa is deteriorating rapidly in corrupt practices both in government and in the private sectors of the economy. This act of corruption is badly affecting the prices of goods and services, and it is affecting the value of the South African rand.

Despite the fact that some leaders in Africa today are trying so hard to emulate Robert Mugabe of Zimbabwe who wish to live and die in power, the ruling national party of the ANC do not condone such acts of indiscipline and unruly behaviour. It is doing its utmost best to eradicate and expunge such leaders from their party and create national peace and stability. The leaders of the ANC have suffered and struggled so much, and they have become wise men and women with the leadership qualities and attributes of late Nelson Mandela. They cannot be said to be innocent, but they are trying to create a balance between corruption and greed in such a way as not to lead the country into chaos and anarchy.

South African leaders have a deep sense of humility and they are down to earth, and they understood the problems of their people as part of their upbringing. Nelson Mandela has proved that humility is the soul of business and leadership. The leadership and people of South Africa are doing their best to follow their role model and the father of this great nation. Nelson Mandela may have come and gone, but his legacy lasts forever in the hearts and minds of all South Africans and people around the world. Though our leaders are not perfect, they must work harder and strive to become better leaders. There is nothing as good as gooness and good leadership in life. Our leaders must inform themselves that what they sow in South Africa is what they shall reap in this country.

We need our people to show a sense of humility towards the nation and the government. They must imbibe the habit of giving and sharing, and stop the habit of criticizing the government unnecessarily but constructively. People must stop to cry wolf over the evils of apartheid, because the kind of life where people feed from rubbish dumps or rubbish dump trucks was not a common sight during the days of apartheid white minority rule. The type of evils, crime, and violence now experienced in South Africa today, the insecurity of lives and properties is quite different from what existed in South Africa during the apartheid era, except the evils and violence committed against the black people during the days of apartheid.

The rate of crime and violence, indiscipline in society, insecurity of lives and properties, and poverty are some of the things that are very worrisome, annoying, and something we must all lament about, and should never be allowed to happen in the newfound freedom and democracy under majority rule. Laziness is not part of the African culture and heritage. Africans have no culture of feeding from the bin no-matter how poor such families might be. In Africa, only mad people feed from the bin because the government of such nations do not cater for the needs and wellbeing of mentally disabled or retarded people. South Africa is not one of such African nations. We know such nations in Africa which does not care for its people or mentally retarded or disabled people despite the fact that some of them are oil and mineral producing nations. Freedom and democracy is not a celebration of poverty and backwardness.

Freedom is power to move forward and do great things in life. It is about empowerment and a celebration of hope for all mankind with the will power to make a better world order, and to give hope and joy to the teeming population. It is about self-determination to rise from grass to grace.

Mandela and many great people on earth today, including the vast majority of ANC leaders rose from grass to grace. They never gave up hope and worked so hard and made the necessary sacrifices to ensure that they rise along with their people to make life more meaningful and pleasant. This is not something that can be done overnight, but it is a task that must be done as soon as possible through dynamic strides as it is done in Europe and America. A good social welfare system is the key to elimination of poverty and the only way to ensure overnight a better life for all South Africans. Such a social welfare system cannot be effective if there is corruption, unnecessary crime and violence in society. It is not healthy for people who refuse to work and contribute to national growth and development.

The kind of situation where people and criminals are deliberately trying to derail the efforts of government and also some people feeding from the bin or rubbish dumps as if they were hopeless or helpless is not the kind of freedom or democracy people fought and died for to make South Africa free. South Africa is predominantly occupied with mechanized farmlands with so much food production and agro-allied industries. This is supposed to lead to industrial growth and development and not to poverty and under-development.

South Africa is feeding the Southern African region, most other African nations, Europe, America, Australia and Brazil with food export. It is not the least a hungry nation. If the cameramen, crew and correspondents of the 'eTv' in South Africa were humane people, such a media should have used their influence to bring trucks loaded with food aids as donations to these poor people and film this good gesture as a symbol of hope, instead of bringing in the cameras to film these hopeless scenes. This is why the United States of America and some first world nations are very different from most other nations of the world. United States is a nation and a people and government that care more about helping humanity than destroying it. United States is a nation with a human heart and not a nation that rejoices in the plights and sufferings of other people and nations. It is defender of the weak and the helpless on earth.

Our poor people are not hungry for 'eTv' cameras in South Africa, but for food. This is the problem with the media in Africa. They make so much money on the pains and miserable news in humanity, but they cannot use this money to help resolve the problems in our lives and feed the poor. They find problems rather than solutions to world problems and crises. They mostly behave and act like prophets of doom. This should not be the case with media and news coverage. We should not only seek for helplessness and hopelessness at the cost of the human blood. We must not place profit before humanity.

I remember an incident on the Grand Parade in Cape Town, when a Somalia man who was my friend shot a Nigerian man who was also my personal friend over girlfriend issues. I personally called the cops, ambulance and the media to the scene of the incident. They media came very late to the crime scene. The only question they kept asking me and shouting at the top of their voices was, 'Where is the blood...., where is the blood?' Like scavengers, they used their cameras to search for the human blood split in the scene of incident. Without blood, there is no news coverage. They are more interested in the human blood than in the salvation of mankind and good news.

Since it is agreeable that South Africa is not a hungry nation, the government must try to ensure that every South African is assured and guaranteed not less than three square meals daily. We know that there is no sane person on earth who would prefer to feed from rubbish dumps if they were not truly hungry. The real danger behind all these is that a hungry man is an angry man, and a hungry mind is a criminal and violent mind.

These negative influences in society are assumed to be created by the third-force who is perceived to be pleased to see us hungry. These forces if they truly exist must not encourage most South Africans to feel hopeless and helpless as if the apartheid era was better than the pro-democracy era. The third force must forget about the mistakes of the past, and bury the hate and anger associated with racism. The so called third force if it really exist must see every poor and ordinary South Africans as their brothers and sisters of the same sword, and they must do their utmost best to make South Africa a better place to live. They should invest their efforts in the fight against crime and violence in society and the eradication of poverty in our national life.

They must make genuine efforts to meaningfully invest their resources and time in the life of the new South Africa. They must not hold back all they benefited from the apartheid regime, or conserve their wealth. They must create an environment devoid of crime and violence in their fight not to make the government of South Africa look like an incompetent demon-crazy.

A change of government involves a general political participation of all South Africans of every colour or race, so that together we can all work together to build a better South Africa. The ANC preaches this theme in their election manifesto as a slogan. The government should encourage all South Africans to join political parties for political participation of all colours and race. Political participation involves majority rule and not race or colour rule. It is not a contest or power sharing or power tussle between the Zulus or the Xhosas. It is not a power tussle between white, coloured and black South Africans. Majority rule does not mean black majority rule, but majority rule of all South Africans of every colour, tribes and race merged into one South Africa.

Power tussle between race, colour or tribe is not the best way to change the government in a truly democratic order. South Africa belongs to everyone of every colour and race. One way of changing the government is to join the political order and belong to any political party of your choice. Play active roles in politics and help to empower those you feel can make South Africa a better place. White and coloured people must join the ANC and have a voice and power in the ruling party. People should not align themselves to political parties on racial lines, colours or tribes. This will create disunity in this great nation. This unholy divide can be seen in the politics of Western Cape and the rift between the Zulus and the Xhosa people, or other elements in our political other in various provinces.

There is need also for serious political reforms by creating two national parties for all South Africans where everyone of every race are free to belong to both political parties on equal terms without regards to colour or race. One way of doing this is the abolition of the existing political parties and start on a fresh slate in other to have the best minds, brains, and the best people in South Africa to lead the nation to a greater future on merit. Leadership should be on merit and not based on those who fought for freedom or opportunity seekers.

This is one way of encouraging political participation in South Africa. This kind of two party systems will encourage excellence, merit and ensure that the best brains rule the nation. Leadership will be based on merit because people are sick and tired of freedom parties or political parties that existed on racial line, and based on the past historical structures. It is time to move forward and allow the ANC and NP or whatever old political party that existed in the past to rest in peace. Real competition and challenges are built on new dispensations and fresh challenges in other to progress into a brand new order.

South Africans deserve a political order of the future for future generations of South Africans, and the present generation. It needs hopeful scenes of life, the kind of hope Mandela gave to us, and we must all discourage these deplorable conditions of life and abominable crimes as a people. What hurts a single South African hurts the entire nation. What good happens to a single South African is the good of a nation. The image of every South African child is an image of the nation, good or bad images. South Africa must become a nation after that ensures that anything bad that happens to any single South African will never happen again; though certain things are unavoidable. Let us try to minimize and avoid unholy incidents that are avoidable and deliberately meant to destroy the future of this great nation.

The South African media has a lot to do for the good of society and they must encourage hopeful scenes, hopeful news, and give hope to the nation through progressive and responsible journalism. The legacies of Mandela and his ideals must be promoted by the media in South Africa as part of our culture and national heritage. The media must deviate and discourage focus on mostly the negative aspects in society and help create solutions to South Africa problems. Good news brings hope, while bad news brings despair.

It is a high time the South African media should ignore bad scenes, bad news, crime and violence and create the kind of journalism that will make meaningful changes and a great difference in making South Africa the crown jewel of Africa. This nation deserves to be painted in lovely beautiful colours of a progressive, peaceful, and thriving rainbow - nation. In this way, there will be hope and people will be encouraged to do good things in society so that their names can be heard and have meaning in life. Bad news is created by bad people in society while good news is created by good people in the same society. Bad news is not a thing of joy and must be discouraged by the media at all cost.

There is no country on earth that is crime free, and the issue of crime and violence should be an exclusive reserve of the communities where these crimes happen daily. The various communities in South Africa owe Mandela and his legacies the responsibility of ensuring a crime free community which encourages peace, progress, togetherness and love. The various communities must honour people of goodwill and discourage anything that will tarnish the image and wellbeing of their communities. It is the duty of everyone to handle the issues of crime as a community priority with the help of the police and judicial system. South Africans cannot and must never allow the issues of crime and violence to distort the hopes and dreams everyone deserve in our nation. The Mandela dream must linger on to have a free and fair society, simple and just, with togetherness and love.

The police and the judicial system did not create the crimes and violence in our communities. It is some people in our communities. The community which allows crime and violence to happen and prosper among them are to blame for such evils, and they have a moral and civic responsibility to stop these crimes and violence in their communities. They have the choice to decide the fate of their community and decide what they want or need for the common good of society. I believe our various communities can do this. Yes, we can!

For the love of Mandela, and all those who died in the struggle, we have the moral and civic responsibility to identify the unruly characters and criminal elements living amongst us and teach them to become better people in life. We do not need to condemn unruly elements in society, but show them love and let them imbibe the spirit of love. We can do this with punishment and rewards.We must give them useful advice in life, and try our utmost best to turn bad eggs to new leaves. This is one way of honouring the exit of the greatest legend of our time; our ability to change people's lives and make the world a better place to live.

As for those people who have resolved and made the wrong choices of becoming die-hard criminals, we have the moral responsibilities of identifying them in our various communities and bring them to justice. It is important to note that the criminals in any community are not greater than their community in content, value, or in numbers, and they are not more powerful than the community they live. The power and greatness of criminals in any community is determined by the power and greatness the community have given to them.

Any community which encourage crime and violence is a criminal community. Every community must blame itself for its' own crimes and woes, and such a community must be held accountable for the destruction and deaths in such communities. This is why the police or law enforcement agents find it most difficult to apprehend criminals easily and bring them to justice without the help of the community. This is what the issues of community policing is all about. The community must help the police to help them in the fight against crime and violence. The police and the communities must work together as partners in progress in the fight against crime and violence.

The community, police, government, and the media are partners in progress. The more the South African media focus their attention on incidents of crime and violence, the more the society become involved in more crimes and violence in other to receive attention. It makes people feel that crime and violence is the answer to their problems. It creates a sense of insecurity of life and properties. It turns criminal minds to heroes and legends.

The security system and network should be expanded in secrecy with undercover cops and undercover private security agents in such a way that criminals do not know who is who in the society. It is better to turn the current sea of visible policing and security industry to undercover agents as part of the society and made part of the community. This will help to infiltrate the dark shadows of crime and violence in this country and identify offenders even before such crimes are committed. In this way, it will be like the case of Russia and Germany where it proves difficult for criminals to identify the good or bad guys amongst men. In this way, it will be most difficult for criminals to operate freely as they do, and they will live in fear for their lives more than they terrorize people in their communities.

In a community where no one knows who is the police, secret agents or security agents, crime and violence will become something people are afraid to do. This will help create a more effective and competent crime intelligence service. It is time to terrorize the criminals in South Africa as if the police and security agents were human drones, surveying the activities of these criminals, identifying them, become part of them, and strike them down. In this way, criminals will not know what happened to them. They will be in jail even before having the opportunity of creating their crimes and violence.

This is the key to the solutions of South Africa crimes and violence in society. The law enforcement agencies must be a thousand times effective and smarter than the criminals in South Africa in other to bring them to justice. In this way, it will be easier to identify the criminal elements in the society, including the good or bad cops in our security system. Community policing must have its rewards which will encourage people to give useful information to the police.

The shame of crime and violence in our society can be seen in the ways criminal news items are broadcasted daily in our news bulletins. Such negative news about our country discourages foreign business investments that will help create jobs and make South Africa a better place to live. Crime and violence is a big blow to the hospitality and tourism industry.

Imagine an incident where a famous and disabled Olympian is being charged for the murder of his girlfriend in the news. According to the Olympian, he said he had thought his girlfriend was an intruder. This kind of excuse to own guns and shoot at people is enough to teach us the lessons of our lives. This is the lesson of gun ownership and the insecurity of lives and properties that play games in the minds of every South African because it is not just a game, it is a matter of reality, and a serious case of life and death.

This is the lesson of what crime and violence can do in society to create demons out of saints. Whether the Olympian was right or wrong, the truth remains that in a climate of crime and insecurity of lives and properties, no one can predict the future. A violent society is a violent future.

Another incident was that of gang rape and gruesome murder of the raped girl at the time when South Africa hosted the soccer "Africa Cup of Nations". These kinds of crimes and incidents in the news items are created by those who do not love us as a people. The more our children are raped and killed, the more society and communities must be blamed for allowing such incidents to happen. This is a very serious incident that society and communities must never tolerate.

Never..., never, and never again should such incidents be allowed to happen in South Africa. It should be treated as acts of terrorism and aggression against the South African people.

We must come together as a people and as a nation and defend our country from those evil elements in society. We must create situations and circumstances that will help encourage local or foreign investments for the common good of this country we all love so much. Every South African must be made part of the law enforcement agency and adequately compensated through legislation to have financial rewards for useful information regarding incidents of crimes and violence. This will help increase their standard of living and make them useful citizens of this great nation. It is better to invest in the lives of all South Africans in the fight against crime and violence than to invest in military hardwares that are just idling away and does no immediate good to the saftety and security of lives and properties.

During negotiations for peace and one South Africa, Mandela used to argue that there is no need to negotiate or compromise the issues of unity, togetherness and love of all South Africans as one nation. He argued that the unity of all South Africans is a task that must be done. He felt that it was easier to understand one another and come together as one people than to assume that we cannot live together to build a better South African.

He pursued the legacy of understanding, togetherness and love, and the need to compromise our various interests, colour and creed and build together a better country for all inhabitants of this land. He knew that any compromise based on equal rights and justice was better than any compromise based on justice for all. He knew that if it was about justice for all, such justice will never be realized in the life of all South Africans in the struggle for freedom.

Mandela was wise enough to know that true justice is hard to find in human lives and that it is something that can never be realized in human ways and means of life. This was why he opted during negotiations with the apartheid regime for justice for the nation and not for justice in individual lives. He believed that justice for the nation will ensure individual justice for all. In this way, never, never, and never again will there be domination of one race by another, and with all South Africans living together in peace and harmony.

Justice for a nation was greater than justice for individual lives which in itself was a very difficult task. Whether realistic or unrealistic our justice system might seem, one thing was clear that it was better to understand each other as people from different race and background, and meet each other half-way in other to move forward in the building of a free and just society. Justice for all South Africans and social justice is a duty we owe everyone through a social welfare system that caters for the needs of everyone. This is something that is realistic and attainable as it is done in the Republic of Ireland.

The issue of justice or social justice is a very complex case and situation spanning over many decades and centuries of human abuse not only during the apartheid regime, but in human lives. Life history has shown us that man has the wickedness of the spirit. Mandela helped us all with all his wisdom to create a balance between the past and the future, and help create a vision that will lead to a better tomorrow. This is the fact that togetherness and love conquers all boundaries. Mandela made it possible for people to love their enemies and embrace their worst nightmares in life. His leadership is the light of hope we all need to make a better future. Jesus Christ has shown us the light, and Nelson Mandela has carried this lamp of God to show us the way to a brighter future for all mankind.

Nelson Mandela was a man who believed that it was better to move forward than to remain backwards. He believed that it was better to be hopeful in life than being hopeless. One way of doing this was to compromise, love, and hope and strive in the process to create a new brand world order based on understanding, togetherness and love to do good for all humanity. We are the captains of our ship. We are the masters of our acts and deeds.

There is a great difference between a superman and a super-heart, and Mandela was not only a superman but a super-heart. He combined both virtues together and forgave all his enemies and ensured that his enemies dined with him on the high table. He became a protector of the weak and meek, the poor and the rich, and he ensured that life is a gift human beings must appreciate and celebrate for the good of society.

Mandela appreciated the fact that no one was perfect, and he used this wisdom to ensure that no one was worthy of condemnation by anyone. He was sympathetic with our hopes, personal views, as well as our individual hopes and dreams, and he ensured that everyone in South Africa has a right to self determination in life. He was a man of many values and virtues. He was the father of modern times.

Mandela was a man who ensured that what is right or wrong is not a matter of human judgment based on sentiments and human egos. He knew that right or wrong was a matter of circumstance or situation beyond human understanding and judgment. It was a matter of morality and self mortification. He knew that good things don't come easy and sacrificed his life to ensure that we learn from him the lessons of life. He has taught us that pains and sacrifices have its rewards.

Mandela was aware that there were negative influences in society, but never for once, and never did he focus his mind on the negative influence in society. He remained steadfast, hopeful and very promising. He believed in South Africa and on South Africans to deliver the goodies that fulfils the promise of true independence and democracy.

He knew that most negative plots happen at a time when hope is near. This is why negative things keep happening when the eyes of the world are focused on South Africa. But South Africans must not be shaken but strengthen itself with resolve to stand strong and firm for that which is morally just. We must learn to to our utmost best in life and hope for what tomorrow will bring.

The truth is that the people in the areas where these negative impacts on society are taking place are not doing South Africa proud, and they are hurting the good image of society. They are destroying their own future. Society belongs to the community and not to the government. If the communities are bad, very bad things will happen in those bad communities. That is why there is so much bad news from those communities who are curators of bad events.

By allowing negative things to happen in their communities, and by damaging the good image of South Africa, it is hard for foreign investors to feel safe enough to invest in the lives of the people. Who is the loser? We are all the losers. Such bad communities are the biggest losers because no meaningful investments, job creation, and good things will take place where bad things happen. Nobody would wish to open factories or industries where there are crimes and violence. No builders would want to go into property business and estates in such bad areas. This is why the crimes and violence created in certain communities must become the problems of those communities. They must decide what they want in their communities. That is their problems and not the problem of government or other people. Communities have a right to decide their own destiny.

But we must refuse as communities and as a people to become losers in the land of our ancestors. We must not bow down to crime and violence in our communities. We must not be afraid of those who seek to hurt us and our children. We must wake up from slumber and come together as a community to decide our future. We must stand together in unity to crush the evils in our communities. We must be united together and expel all criminal and evil elements in our communities. We must ensure that there is no place for evils to hide in our communities.

Evil elements can run to the sun, and the sun will burn them up on that day. They can run to the moon, the moon will melt them down on that day. We are winners and we must keep on winning over crime and violence same way Mandela and others helped to win our freedom for us as a nation. Our victory must not be a victory for the blacks over the coloured and white people. It must be a victory of all South Africans and our communities over the forces of darkness in our lives. It must be a victory over crime and violent attacks in our various communities. We must continue the struggle to keep this victory alive in our long walk to freedom. Every community must begin a long walk to freedom. We must today join and team up with such legends like Desmond Tutu in our long walk to eradicate crime and violence in our communities and society. This is a task that must be done! It is a necessary choice we have to make.

If there are no foreign investors and investments to help create jobs for us and for our children, everyone suffers the fate, and the economy cannot grow at the pace it should do. Negative influence does not help create jobs in any society. Any capital investment founded on the environment of crime and violence is sure to liquidate its' assets and fold up under the negative influence of crime and violence. It does not encourage small business growth and development. Every negative act in society by anyone is a step in the wrong direction, a step backwards in the social economic growth and development of South Africa. A thousand kilometres journey begins with one single step; and it is a national duty and obligation for every South African to take every single right step in the right direction for the common good of all South Africans and children yet unborn.

Finally, we all know that we are not perfect people, and that there is no way in life we can live perfect lives. We all know we have done some wrong things in life and in society one way or the other. Yet, we all know that every human action is controllable and that the choices we make in life will decide our future. What we sow in the field of life, is the harvest we will reap in those aspects of life. Since we are not perfect people, at least we can try to control our thoughts, our words and deeds. At least we can try as South Africans to become better people. No one can blame us for trying our best because we have only one nation, one country, and only one South Africa. An only bubblegum does not get lost in the teeth.

Joe Odiboh

Chapter 2
The Part to Peace and Nation Building

The path to truth, reconciliation, and peaceful coexistence in South Africa is not an easy task to accomplish because truth is as bitter as the bitter cola-nuts. The truth is that the problems in this country must not be left to the singular efforts of government to remedy with a magic wand. There is no government on earth that has the magic wand to make miracles happen in every human life. We must not forget where we are coming from, our past and our history; and we must allow these virtues to become the strength we need now and tomorrow to make amends. We need this knowledge and wisdom from our historical past in helping to resolve all our current problems, knowing and bearing in mind that we cannot solve all these problems at once without any storm and stress, and without igniting the burning flames in the devil's door.

It is something that requires the efforts of every citizen and visitors to the land. The problems in South Africa belong to all South Africans as individuals and as a nation, and together everyone must make meaningful contributions to make South Africa great for all and for the common good of society. We know that if over the years dreams die, our people have kept intact their dreams to see a free and fair South Africa which belongs to all, free and just, united and strong, and a country free from racial bias and any form of discrimination.

The issue of racial discrimination is not simply about colour or race, but about social equality, economic empowerment, and equal social conditions of life, equal opportunities to a basic standard of living for all South Africans, irrespective of colour, race or creed. This is not a problem that must be addressed by only the government, but also by all those who helped create such conditions of inequality. Some of these people can be found and identified among our communities. Even so, we know that there are millions of South African white people and many other Europeans and Americans, including a lot of people around the world who fought against the institution of the apartheid regime as an unjust system and stood all the way with our black and coloured brothers and sisters to set our country free. We must appreciate all these people and learn to appreciate everything good in our lives.

It is equally fair that those who supported and benefited profitably from the apartheid system should not sit back and look, but they must honestly and sincerely help facilitate a system for rationalization of the wealth in society necessary to turnaround the fortunes of this great nation. They can do this by investing and making the necessary sacrifice that will guarantee their children and future generations a better and fruitful future. They must always see South Africa as their country and become part of the social, political and economic life of this great nation.

They must stop to act as minority groups and consider themselves as part of the larger community. They must not leave the leadership of South Africa to the ANC or majority group. They must become patriotic and believe that all South Africans are the same one big family. They must not allow their lives to be ruled by colour or race, but by the greater good everyone can do for this nation. They must believe in themselves as possessing the power to become the heroes and heroines of this great nation. They must believe that they have the will power to win the mandate of the people of this nation to rule this country and lead us to the part of glory and greatness.

As Nelson Mandela would rightly say, that it was better to compromise and understand each other's needs, hopes and dreams than to inherit the country in tatters. So saying, the future of this country do not only belong to us, it belongs to all our children and future generations. This is the time to begin the long walk to freedom and free the future generations from poverty, backwardness, and from crime and violence. The tide is turning, and the weather is becoming a storm which we must not allow to overturn our boats and wreck our lives. We must not wait to bemoan our future.

This is the time for nation building. Speaking of nation building does not simply mean creating more shopping malls, building and renovation the Metro-rail or train stations, building bus tracks, or construction of roads and bridges. These are very far from the acts of nation building because a nation cannot simply be built with rocks and stones. Stones and rocks are innocent natural objects, and we must not focus on using or abusing their innocent nature to blindfold the real agenda in human lives. True nation building starts from our hearts and minds. It is very easy to destroy rocks and stones, but it is not easy to destroy our hearts and minds, our hopes and dreams.

The real task of nation building lies with every individual efforts in making this country a better place to live. It is not only about commerce and industry; it also involves building our mentalities, social reconstruction, patriotism, civic rights and obligations, political participation, togetherness and love.

is called community service.

Without mincing words, most of the white people of this
great nation who in their hearts know that they benefited from
the injustice of the apartheid system, must not be content with
their good or better standard of living which they inherited
from the apartheid era. They must think about their future and
future generations to come. They must start to take stock of
the future of this country and become part of government and
national agenda. Apartheid and racial discrimination is over,
dead and buried. The time is now to become part of history by
what they can do to make South Africa a better place to live,
and with a society that is free and just. They must help to build
a society free from racial bias, crime and violence.

Such people should use the life and death of Nelson
Mandela as a legacy to transform their thoughts and deeds.
They should understand that since Mandela did not live
forever, social injustice in South Africa will not last forever.
They must use this period of sober reflection to reflect on their
lives and reflect on the future. They should reflect on what
good they can do for this country and what good this nation
can do for their children and future generations.

As Mandela would rightly say, 'Never, never, and never
again shall we witness in this country the domination of one
race by another'. This means that no white or black race,
Indians or colour must dominate each other in ways and
means of livelihood. In this context, he further explained that
'freedom, equal rights and justice in a democratic order was
meaningless if people go to bed and sleep without food in their
stomachs, and with no place to call a home and rest their
heads'.

This kind of reasoning and understanding is what we all
need to ensure better life for all. This is why we all owe a duty
to South Africa as a nation and to ourselves as a people to

ensure a better social welfare system that caters for all our needs. We owe a duty to the Mandiba legacies by undoing the ills in society. We should endeavour to assist the government to undo the problems created by the apartheid regime; through understanding, sacrifice, togetherness and love. By doing this, it will enable all South Africans keep alive their hopes and dreams.

Every South African of every colour or race has hopes and dreams, and these hopes and dreams cannot be fully realized under storms and stress in their lives. It is not an easy thing to find joy and happiness in inequality and unfairness. This implies that since the evils of apartheid was defeated and drowned in the Cape Point, between the Indian and Atlantic Ocean, we must create a government legislation to guarantee every South African child a better life and a better tomorrow from Western Cape to the Eastern or Northern Cape. We can do this by helping one another in whatever way we can and by any means.

The inequality and all those strings and attachments associated with the apartheid policy and regime is sure to fall with its system. How these strings and attachments will finally vanish into the thin air is a question of moral issue. Only time will tell how reasonable we are to use the exit of our father, Nelson Mandela to make life meaningful for all South Africans. We can do this through loving and caring for each other's needs. Our people who will never stop dreaming. It is the dream of our people to see everyone having equal rights and justice, equal share of the nation's resources, economic growth and development.

This does not imply the economic growth and development of only a cross section of society, but of all South Africans of every race, colour and creed, irrespective of social economic background or parental up-bringing. A citizen of this country does not need to be a white person or the son and daughter of politicians to have a better life in this country. Everyone is entitled to aspire to greater heights in life and a future which is securely guaranteed. Good standard of living is a right and not a privilege for all our people. This right to a better life must be the first priority in government legislation. Any political structure that does not expel poverty and poor standard of living from our lives is a wasted political order and does not represent the yearnings of our people.

It is the yearning of every person in this country that the great hopes and aspirations which over the years we have held so dear to our hearts will be fully realized and accomplished without any particular person or race having a better life than the order, and with true integration process of every colour or race living side by side as neighbours with each other in the same communities without racial divide, or informal settlements still in existence. Until that day, when everyone live side by side without black or coloured settlements still in existence, South Africa will still be seen as a segregated country where unity is far from diversity. A country divided against it-self cannot stand the test of time. This division can be seen in the difference between the life in informal settlements and the ghettoes in comparism with life in other surburbs inhabited by those lucky to experience a better life in this country.

The exit of our legend and icon, Nelson Mandela should bring us together as a country with unity in diversity. In this way, our days in this country will not be like that of the antelopes, which tried in vain to serve the purpose of the springboks, and failed woefully as steak to meet with the salivating demands of the appetite. We must use the great loss of Mandela in our lives to continue to dream bigger and greater dreams. It must be the dream of all South Africans to be united as one nation, one country, and one destiny. This is the dream of the founding fathers of freedom and democracy, and it is a task that must be done if the name, 'South Africa' must continue to have meaning before the rest of the world.

It is no use pretending that all is well, and that we are strongly united together. Since we know that things are far from being well for the vast majority of our people, we should feel challenged to do better and live better lives. We cannot simply pretend to be united together for the sole reason of a rugby or football soccer match. It is not about the black and coloured people being encouraged to drink Carling 'Black Label Lager Beer' during soccer matches, or the white and coloured communities being encouraged to drink 'Amstel Lager Beer' during rugby or cricket matches. It is about unity is strength in togetherness and love.

Living the way things are at the moment in South Africa is like self-deceit. I know that the vast majority of the black and coloured communities are segregated and marginalized, which has resulted in the high rates of crimes and violence in these marginalized communities. The issue of unemployment is one sensitive issue that is destroying the social lives and conditions in these communities, and it is making them hot spots for unruly behaviours and Calcutta Republics for the Towers of Babel.

Living in South Africa, we cannot pretend that we do not know the difference in the standard of living of some particular race if we compare it to some other race, especially to the black race. We know the great difference in the various areas of the society, depending on which colour or race of people are living in such areas, their social economic background, conditions of life in those areas, and which cannot in any way be compared with other areas.

These kinds of diversities make the work of government even harder in attempting to bridge the gap in the social economic conditions of life of our people. The government have done so much for the people, but help is also needed from everyone to help compliment the good efforts of government. This is the only way forward in building a free and fair society, united and strong. This is the only way to avoid division in society, and avoid chaos and anarchy in near future.

The division in society is growing by the clock; racial consciousness and awakening is getting worse and more dangerous in the battle to correct the ills and social divide in society. Gaps cannot be bridged between race and colour if segregation gaps and social conditions get wider from day to day. The escalating high cost of living is not helping the situation. It is no use uniting together as a people like hypocrites for sports, a Rugby or Soccer match in front of television screens, without uniting together politically, socially, and economically as one people in one nation with one aim and one common goal. Victory in sports is not victory for individuals to have a better life.

Any unity that is not of togetherness and love is like a basket full of rotten tomatoes. These rotten tomatoes will be thrown away and grow into weeds and thorns in society. This is ironically the negative things we all see in South Africa today, choking the society, stinging innocent citizens like bees, and threatening day by day to tear apart the common bonds that unite us together as a people.

That is why some people are living in joy and peace, while others are living in sorrow, tears and blood. Innocent children and babies are being raped and killed in some areas; people are being robbed, killed and murdered in cold blood. Gang wars and taxi wars are in the offensive, drug wars and immorality have blinded some communities, and there is a general insecurity of lives and properties in most areas inhabited especially by black and coloured communities.

In the midst of all these, life has become as cheap as biltong. Violence, irresponsibility, unruly behaviour and disrespect for anyone by anyone have become a culture in society, something that has never been, and should never be the culture in South Africa. Children are growing up with very bad influence in society, something that is not of African culture or nature in African family or traditional system. Children no-longer respect their elders, and people no-longer respect their leaders, something that is alien in the way our mothers conceived and gave birth to us as Africans.

All these unholy abnormalities in South Africa are being reflected in the music, art, theatre, and industry where violence is the theme of labour unions. The influence of American Hollywood cinema, rap music, ghetto life in the USA and in South America, and drug wars in Mexico have found their ways into black and coloured communities in South Africa with our people thinking that we are Americans, and forgetting we are Africans. As Africans, we must act and do things like Africans, a system of respect, dignity, togetherness and love. Africans are not known to be drug dealers and addicts.

It is therefore understandable and tolerable among our people to see most Africans living the way they are in this country, because they are black people being ruled mostly by black leaders. This kind of thought is the frame of mind most people carry in their hearts as South Africans, and we use these thoughts to drag ourselves backwards and make life more difficult in this country. We must not think or reason negatively about ourselves and our future. We must not fail our future generations by behaving as though our people and our leaders cannot raise us to greater heights in life. We must believe in ourselves and our leaders to ensure for us greater prospects in life.

As Africans, we must stop to think and behave as if freedom and democracy is a right to spoil and ruin everything being done by our Africans leaders in the ANC and other political parties. We must stop to think and behave as if we can only respect ourselves, behave properly and respect a government if South Africa becomes Europe with European leaders. We must stop to behave as though we are not prepared for freedom and democracy and that if a labourer is not flogged by the master, he will not work properly to respect the master's will. Our African leaders in this country unlike most other African countries are humane people who are not ready to place themselves as masters but as public servants to the people. This is something to respect and not something we must abuse and take advantage of in doing all the wrong and negative things in society.

We must understand that it is not the government that is erecting shacks and Wendy-houses in the various locations and informal settlements, instead; the government is faced with the difficult task of demolishing these illegal structures in the provision of proper housing and facilities. Former President Thabo Mbeki and Jacob Zuma tried to move the country forward, but their efforts were frustrated not by the white people in this nation, but by our own black brothers and sisters they tried so hard to bring better life to their door-steps. We must stop to cry wolf over corruption in government while in our hearts we are more corrupt than these leaders. The issue of corruption is a national tragedy and we must fight this as a national problem in every sphere of our national life. That is how to fight corruption. We cannot fight corruption with biased minds by witch-hunting certain people simply because they are placed in positions of authorities. It is about fighting corruption holistically as a national agenda in a way that no one is above the law.

We must not forget that it is not the government that is raping children and women in the communities and killing innocent people, instead it is faced with the responsibility of spending millions of the tax payers' money in protecting the children and women in the society, and bring the criminals to justice. The government is not murdering and assassinating people like what we see in some other nations of the world, instead it is tolerant and understanding in its battle to rid society of these menaces. The government is not perfect because as humans we are not perfect. It is doing its utmost best to better the lives of the people in this great nation.

As citizens of this nation, we owe our country a great responsibility by meeting the government half way through in the betterment of the society, and in what contributions we make to make South Africa a better place for us and for all our children. We must learn to face the truth and reality by not blaming the government for crimes they did not commit. We must stop to demonize the government and use our community forums to fight crimes and the evils in our communities. The people who are doing all the negative things in society live among us in our various communities. We know them very well because they are part of us. They are our fathers and mothers, brothers and sisters, our sons and daughters.

It is for us as people in the various communities to identify these people and rid them of all the negative things they are doing to destroy our communities and bring them to justice. We must understand that as communities where these evils are being committed, we are the ones at the receiving end of these crimes and violence, and all the negative things in society as they affect us as a people. The problems in our communities are our problems and we have a moral responsibility to deal with them positively the same way we deal with problems in our families. We must start to appreciate our leaders and stop character assassination or disrespect of our leaders. We must start to appreciate every effort of government because the parliament will not initiate any law in government policies to harm its own people.

They can do that in some countries or the rest of African nations, but definitely not in this country. South Africans need to crawl out of their shells and go into adventures in other African countries and continents around the globe to see how life is outside their country in other to become exposed, enlightened, more sociable and appreciate the good efforts of government in their own country. It is a high time our people must put a total and final full stop to the negative acts and deeds in South Africa and stop dragging to the mud all good efforts of government being run by our leaders. We must learn to criticize constructively and advice ourselves on what solutions we think are reasonable and feasible in solving our problems and national crises.

Every South African must learn how to think of the problems in South Africa and find lasting solutions to these problems through community forums. The various communities must bring the solutions to our national problems before the attention of government for deliberation and legislation. The problems of every single South African merit deliberation in the national assembly and parliament, and it must be resolved without much ado. This is the work and task of government in problems and crises resolution in society. People must be free to cry out and say their problems aloud.

This is what freedom of speech is all about. Freedom of speech is not freedom of stupid, foolish and careless words in society. I believe that the way we embraced freedom foolishly and carelessly as a people without thinking what positive roles and responsibilities we must play as a people in the new democratic order, is the reason why we keep doing the wrong things we are doing in South Africa, same way as we have done in the rest of African nations.

By doing all these negative things in this country as Africans, we are not encouraging other people of other races in this country to respect our people and our leaders; neither are we encouraging them to face up to their challenges, duties and obligations to the nation. We know that some white people owe South Africa a great deal, and they also know this fact. While they did a lot to develop the country for themselves and their children, they are ready to do more for the future if we all behave and act responsibly.

This is why they are very quiet and patient, watching us closely and monitoring our activities to see what direction we are leading the country, knowing they cannot and will not allow us to destroy their future. They are ready and prepared to help make South Africa great if we as individuals and as Africans show good and sterling qualities as a people. I believe they are prepared to merge together with us as brothers and sisters if we behave responsibly as Africans with the spirit of 'Ubuntu'. *We cannot preach the spirit of 'Ubuntu' and act out like Mobutu*.

The white community cannot live in the same community where their children and daughters will be raped, killed and mutilated by people of other race. They are not prepared to live with people in the coloured communities where drugs and crimes is prevalent. No particular race is free from incidence of crime and drugs, but how we allow our bad habits to destroy our various communities is the issue at stake. Though some of them take drugs as a habit, but they have not allowed the incident of drugs addiction to tear their communities' apart, same way as it has done in the coloured and black communities. Let us encourage the other races to live among us and be part of our lives in the black and coloured communities. If we do not live together as one in the same communities as mixed race and colour; the incidence of crime will become more explosive in this country.

We have observed that the white people are more conscious of the rule of law, and are more highly organized and law abiding, living in their own world, and seldom allow the negative influence in the black and coloured communities to affect them in their own world in South Africa. For effective integration process to take place for national growth and development, it is imperative therefore that we should create an enabling circumstance to make other races reasonable and wise enough to contribute their quota to making South Africa greater for everyone more than it was for them during the apartheid regime and colonization.

As Africans, poverty is not strange to us. We know that we are tolerant and patient people who work and sacrifice so hard to build a better future for our children. With poverty and long suffering, we have grown up in life to be very strong people who can endure the tribulations of life on this planet. Our strength that has made us great and survivors on earth should not be used by impatient and recalcitrant youths to destroy the good image of the African people.

We have struggled and suffered so much and for so long to bring about freedom and democracy in this country. Those who are dragging the good image of this country to the mud and are committing crime and violence are not people who fought for freedom and democracy in this country; they are opportunity seekers who take advantage of freedom and democracy to demonize our national agenda. These kinds of evil people in our various communities in South Africa must be seen and classified as enemies of the state, because their aim is to bring us sorrow tears and blood. However, in the building of a united front for social gains, political and economic growth and development, we must make a great effort and difference in proving and demonstrating the love we have and share for our beloved nation.

How can we commit so much crimes and violence and destroy a country we love so much, which our people fought and died for? How can we rape, maim and kill our own brothers and sisters, and ruin the good image of our fatherland? Where then is the humanity in us? Where is the spirit of 'Ubuntu'? Is crime and violence our culture and tradition? The spirit of 'Ubuntu' is not the spirit of thieves, robbers, rapists and murderers. It is not the spirit of poverty and backwardness in society. It is the spirit of love, peace, and progress in our land. These are the questions and issues every criminal element must start to reflect on in moral principles before thinking of the evils that they do in this great nation. It is better to live in poverty and humility than to live in shame and disgrace as a thief, rapist, murderer, or baby killer.

Most of the greatest, wisest, and wealthiest Africans today on earth once lived in poverty and humility. Their parents suffered and struggled in life to help them build a better future, and this inspired them to aspire to greater heights in life. I believe the late former President Nelson Mandela, former President Thabo Mbeki, Arch Bishop Desmond Tutu, Kofi Annan, Barrack Obama, Oprah Winfrey, and President Jacob Zuma did not grow up in very rich and affluent homes and families; same with most successful Africans all over the universe.

These people knew the meaning of struggles and suffering, and they were content with the hope and dreams that was the milk of life that flowed in their hearts. Their passion for hopes and dreams is the story of success in life, same with such people like Chief Obafemi Awolowo, Dr. Nnamdi Azikiwe, Kwame Nkrumah, Oliver Tambo, Walter Sisulu, Wole Soyinka, Chinua Achebe, Joe Modise, Steve Biko, Joe Slovo, Frank Okoyo Ekpudu, Dr. Tony B. Bello the food scientist, Sly Edaghese the great journalist, and many others who sacrificed their lives to make the world a better place to live.

This is why we must unite together in the fight and struggle to rid this nation of criminal elements and become a God fearing nation determined in our resolve to create a long and lasting peace, freedom and democracy in our part to greatness where people are free and safe to dream and hope for a better tomorrow. We must draw our strength from our weaknesses in the part to greatness. This is what makes us strong and wise. This is what makes us as Africans great on earth, and not shameful incidence of gangs, rape, stealing, robbery or killing of innocent souls and babies.

It is sad however that in most other African nations, we have learnt how to suffer and be silent, and we have formed the habit of accepting poor African leadership and untold evils, as part of our cultural heritage and upbringing. We have learnt how to honour corruption, admire greed, and respect those with wealth or in positions of authority. As good or bad our ways and cultural upbringing might seem, one thing is certain, that we Africans are not rapists, thieves and murderers by nature. The culture of violence is an alien culture imported and borne out of overt unkindness, envy, or prejudice. We use to be very happy and merry people who are not greedy for wealth or hungry for souls or human blood. We use to have love for each other as one family and respect our elders and leaders of our communities.

Even so, we know we are not perfect, and there have always been and will always be evil people in our society, many of whom are into occult, spiritualists, and witchcraft as a way of furthering their evil intentions. All these evils are different from the current wave of evils we do witness in South Africa today. Only if we re-evaluate our minds and hearts and imbibe this spirit of goodwill, we cannot grow as Africans to become better people and better nations in the face of current globalization. It is a good thing to be identified for what we are as moral people, than what we own as individuals, or for what evils we do as a people in vanity. By doing all these evils in our various communities, we are securing for our children and future generations passports to hell. It is like offering our kids visas to oblivion.

One thing we must understand and accept is the fact that the world being what it is and has always been recognizes us as African people whether or not South Africa is a rainbow nation. It is seen and regarded as a third world country though most parts of South Africa are more developed than most European countries, especially the Eastern Europe where most people still experience poverty, hunger and starvation. No matter how much resources we invest on infrastructures, the world is at ease when most black people are impoverished and live the way they do in this country, because the West think the problems of Africa belongs to Africans.

They believe without questions that poor African leadership is responsible for the African woes and dilemma, an issue that is natural in the African continent. Though we cannot allow poor African leadership and poverty to rule our lives, we must not allow worse evils such as becoming rapists, thieves, crime and violence to become our cultural heritage amidst corruption. These are not noble and responsible replacement for our misplaced priorities in our general conducts and attitudes to life.

The white people in South Africa are living decent lives and are enjoying peace and tranquillity in their respective communities because they chose to live that way and adopted a better life policy for their children. The choices we make in life are what determine the way of life and situations and conditions of life created for our children in our communities. If we choose to live like vampires, we will become vampires in the life of our communities; something that is sure to impact on the lives of our children and future generations. The nature or social conditions of a community is a true reflection of how the people in that community are as a people like flocks of birds with the same feathers. No one in such a community is exempted from the good, the bad and ugly situation in that community.

In communities such as those of the white race in South Africa, they are not raping and killing their children and women, robbing each other on the street the way we do in the black and coloured communities. They do not kill their brothers and sisters or immigrants in their areas. The worse any white man can do in personal anger and frustration with family problems, is to kill members of his family and turn the gun on himself in the usual white man fashion and culture of domestic violence. Even so, these are very rare and isolated incidence which the majority of their people condemn with impunity.

Even if they commit crimes, it is either a whitepaper crime or well-coded crimes done in the civilized way. These are very few and reported incidence which are dealt with by the criminal justice system. The white people are not living recklessly and irresponsibly like we black and coloured people do in South Africa, because they know what good things they want in life for all their people. This is why they are prospering in South Africa, while most of us are living with all the negative things in our communities without shame or sense of reasoning and national disgrace.

Those white people who own the farms are generations of farmers who have worked so hard from one generation to the other to perfect their skills and craftsmanship in ensuring the survival of their farms. They have patience in working and waiting and never gave up hope during difficult times in their lives. They made sacrifices to ensure operation feed the nation of South Africa. They never allowed wealth to get into their heads and become lazy farmers with abandoned farmlands.

Even now that apartheid is gone and over with, they the white people do not have much regrets because the existing system have appreciated their understanding and support.

This is why it is very necessary and important for the African people to respect, appreciate, cherish and support the present political dispensation with goodwill and good intentions in the way we behave ourselves, and we must stop the incidence of crime and violence in society so that we can see the good in this government and reap the rewards of our actions.

We can never reap anything good in life, or from the government by raping and killing innocent children and women, commit violent crimes, and disrespect the government that will provide for us and our families. Nothing good in life comes to a criminal and what you take by force will be taken away from you by force. Those who live by knives and guns will die by knives and guns. That is just the way it is in life with its own set rules and laws of natural justice. What we sow, is what we shall reap in life.

The white minority apartheid regime in South Africa did not only build council houses and improved the conditions of life of the white minority, the government provided them with education, jobs, qualitative social welfare services, good wages, and good quality of life and privileges that enabled them to have a good future in the land they called their own. They lived in South Africa as if they were in Europe or America. They do not live in shacks or Wendy houses like in the ghettoes or informal settlements.

This kind of goodwill from their government of the past is what the African people in government are trying desperately to do for all South Africans irrespective of their colour or race, and many of us are abusing this system instead of using it to positive affirmative action to better our lives. I cannot separate myself from the African people, and I believe that I am one of those African people who have not done South Africa proud.

By abusing the good efforts of government policies and programs of empowerment, we are not encouraging the government to do more by frustrating their efforts. As South

Africans, we must encourage the government in their efforts for the people in a very responsible way, so that the resources used in combating violent crimes and negative influence in society can be re-channelled towards nation building and the provision of good standard of living for the common man. People must understand that they are the ones making the work of government more difficult in South Africa through irresponsible citizenship, and the incidence of crimes and violence in society. We must face this fact and accept responsibility for all our actions. This we can do if we repent from our sinful and evil ways and become better people for a better nation.

Government cannot do everything at once because it has no magic wand to make miracles happen overnight. People must learn to have patience, trust and understanding that good things don't come easy in life. It takes a great deal of time, proper planning and implementation of government plans and policies in development plans and projects. There is no country or government in Africa that is doing anything close to what the South African government is doing for its entire people in consideration of the complex situation of living in peace and harmony without creating a crises that might tear the country apart. It takes the wisest men and women on the face of the earth, including God's guidance to rule a complex country such as South Africa, especially after the apartheid injustice of over three hundred years.

South Africans must learn to appreciate the government, respect its leaders, and help to contribute meaningfully to the social economic growth and development. The leaders in government are as human as every South African, and they have taken upon themselves the responsibilities of riding this country through the greatest storm on earth with great care and caution. They should be appreciated and helped by all onboard the ship to its destination. We must not allow our ship to sink as captains of our nation. We must become good masters of our good destiny.

The progress made in society is not measured by the crime and violence of the people, or simply by the strength of how many houses, roads and bridges are constructed or built for violent and unruly citizens, but by responsible citizenship. It includes how much investment is made in ensuring a qualitative standard of living for all, and provision of the basic human needs that fulfils the hopes and dreams of the people. *These hopes and dreams are not inclusive of crime and violence. The ball of goodwill is now in our court as individuals to play into the goal of love, peace, progress and national growth and development.*

Facilitating our hopes and dreams is something the black majority rule of the ANC in South Africa is trying to do, and we must take into considerations the need to appreciate and compliment this effort if freedom and democracy must have true meaning for all the people of this great nation. We know that it is important for the government to continue in their efforts to focus on improving the quality of life of every single child or anyone proud to be called a South African. Focus is an essential element in life for progress.

This is something the government cannot do effectively by distraction if our children are being raped and killed, and our people are being robbed and killed in cold blood day and night. It is a very difficult thing to make progress under insecurity of lives and properties, when people are violent and chaotic which could lead to anarchy. I sincerely believe chaos and anarchy is not what we need in South Africa. *If we initiate chaos and anarchy in this country, we shall all become sons and daughters of anarchy and be doomed forever.*

There is a great difference between a hungry man and an angry man, but there are no differences between a criminal mind and a criminal element. A criminal is someone with an evil mind and intent to hurt man and humanity. A hungry man is a struggling man battling and working hard to provide for himself and his family. A hungry man is a man with hopes and dreams to conquer hunger and poverty in the family through hard work, discipline and dedication.

There is no difference between a liar, thief, rapist, or murderer. A rapist is not a hungry man but a violent person with the heart of a demon. A hungry man has no strength or the energy to rape or kill anyone, except such an evil person is under the influence of drugs or alcohol and has lost his mind. Even so, there is a great difference between needs and wants in economics. Wants and needs have to do with opportunity cost of something we have to forgo and make the necessary sacrifices to overcome our problems in life.

We know the difficulties people are facing in life, and the problems of unemployment. This should not be used as excuse for criminal activities and violence in society. The time wasted in plotting and planning a crime must be used to plan for creative ideas that enrich human lives. This energy must be used in education, skills development, manpower development, arts, sports and enterprise. An intelligent mind is a creative mind, but a foolish mind is a stupid person who has nothing good to offer humanity. This is the kind of mind which idle people use in sitting around street corners plotting their evils. This is the mind of people who carry guns and knives in their pockets to hurt and harm innocent people in society. Carrying guns and knives in the pocket is the power of fools in their foolish evil activities as cowards in society. Such people are puppets and despots who have failed themselves in life.

The time and mind negatively used for criminal activities must be used for positive thinking and creativity with hopes and dreams to focus on productivity. A tree that does not bear good fruits is usually cut down and cast into fire. People must think which kind of fruits they wish to bear in life. Do you wish to bear the fruits of Nelson Mandela, or the fruits of Osama Bin Laden?

The culture of laziness or moral laxity in people and youths is responsible for the high rates of crime in society. This creates impatience and people who want things to be done now, right now! They behave as though the future is a thing of the past. They want fast and luxurious cars right now. They want to reap where they have not sowed any seed. They think by doing this, they are smart people. Smartness is the ability to rise anytime you fall from the struggles of life to make the world a better place, and make life more meaningful and fruitful.

Smart people are those who can rise industriously from grass to grace. They are people our communities and society can be very proud of for their achievements in life. You cannot stand up boldly and be proud to say you achieved being a rapist, robber, a common thief, house breaker, abuser, murderer, and killer of babies, murderer of children and innocent people. You cannot boast of useless acts and deeds. You cannot boast of being a sinner and a very bad person and bad influence in society. As a typical denizen of Nigeria, I would like South Africans to know that 'NFA' in Nigeria means 'No Future Ambition'. Let us not become people with no future ambitions. Let us become the Bill Gates of South Africa. Let us think and act to be like the youths who created the facebook.

South Africans must be glad that they have a government with good intentions and has made good efforts to provide for the people basic human needs such as housing, free health services and other social welfare services. People are abusing this system and wallowing in laziness and lack of hard work and creativity. Many people have stopped dreaming and started acting irrationally and irresponsibly without future ambitions. They think and believe that their hopes and dreams and their future ambitions is the sole prerogative of government actions, policies and agendas because of freedom and democracy. These are the people who do not understand the true meaning of freedom and democracy, or the role of government in the life of a nation.

This ignorance and frame of mind where hopes and dreams cease to exist in human minds is a deep cut and pain in the ass of government who is under pressure to provide everything free for all its people, especially for the black or coloured communities who were the original victims of social injustice of the past. This pressure of irresponsible demands for free everything makes it difficult for government to justify responsible demands from the irresponsible ones.

Even so, is the problem of recognition of what the government is doing right or doing wrong in their lives. They fail to see what is right from what is wrong and this negative energy is channelled into negative acts and deeds in their words, their thoughts and Acts of the Apostles. Knowing that human wants are insatiable, some people wish to have everything by force.

If the government gives someone an RDP house, the next day another illegal structure will be erected next to the building or at the backyard for other relations or tenants. The person is not satisfied with government housing program, he or she wants free food, free clothing, free water, free electricity, free education, free beer or wine, free gas and cookers, free plates and spoons, free washing machines and Turbo dryers. They wish to ride on the metro rails trains free of charge, and shoplift if freedom and democracy permits stealing in the shopping malls and centres. They wish KFC, McDonalds, Pick n Pay, Hungry Lion, Woolworths, Edgers, Shoprite Checkers, and South African Breweries were free for anyone to have anything free for a good time.

Because of this frame of mind, some people who have no jobs or any means of income, and have no money in their pockets or wallets, wake up every day and spend their time walking around, and window shopping day and night, looking for houses where the owners are at work to break into, looking for people to rob and kill, week by week, month by month, year in and year out under the shadow of temptation and darkness. They wish to either shoplift, break the shop and steal, or rob people to meet their needs. They want to rob the hardworking people of South Africa of their salaries and wages. Some young girls and women want to sleep around and abandon their homes and families. This is the genesis of the petty crimes in this country. People want to reap where they did not work, and rob Innocent to pay the evil King of darkness.

Whereas we know that it was possible for these idle loafers or people to acquire any minor skills such as carpentry, wrist watch repairs, auto mechanic, construction, electrician, plumbing, welding, panel beater, spray painter, driver, fork lift driver, machinist, and those relevant skills that will empower them to get meaningful and gainful employment both in the public and private sector, or start own business as self employed.

Instead of empowering themselves, they waste their days and time on earth window shopping, walking around hopelessly and forgetting that an idle mind is the devil's workshop. Others hang around the streets and street corners in their locations and settlements while other people are at work. They hang around, waiting for the workers to return with their wages so that they can rob and mug them of their wages and hard earned incomes. This is what happens in the black and coloured settlements and making life unbearable for the ordinary South Africans. At the end, we blame the government for our idleness and crimes against humanity.

These idle minds rob and kill people for their money, wallets, jewelleries, wrist watches, or cellular phones so that they can smoke drugs and drink beer with the money. When they are caught or killed in this evil act, they blame their crimes on the government and on unemployment. This is the habit and culture of certain evil people in the coloured and black communities in South Africa. This kind of dangerous way of life is a national shame and community disgrace. This is something that must stop. The community must rise up and face up to this challenge to rid their communities of these kinds of incidents and idleness.

The most shameful aspect of the housing program of government is that some of the people who have been given RDP houses by the government, reason negatively in a way that a hungry man faced with difficulties on how to survive in life and cater for the needs of their family cannot eat or drink RDP houses. Those without RDP houses feel that they cannot sleep on newly reconstructed roads and bridges, or in newly built shopping plazas. They feel that it is very hard for them to see these development efforts of government if their own lives are not built and reconstructed to meet with their hopes and dreams.

Having a house is one thing, but catering for the needs of the family is a different issue entirely. Making a country more beautiful is one thing, but being unable to have a life and live like a human being in that beautiful country is another problem in the lives of most South Africans. This is where a viable and effective social welfare system comes into the rescue in ensuring a better life for all. This is the task of government for the common good of all South Africans.

This is the reality problem with candid reality check that is torturing the hearts and minds of most South Africans. Most black people tend to see the beauty and development in South Africa in the eyes of an alien, because the majority of them personally own nothing that guarantees them a better life. Our people feel alienated from progress in their own fatherland.

Many of them feel they are not part of it, hungry, jobless, penniless, homeless and helpless. There is no one in South Africa or a child who would wish to grow up in shacks and Wendy houses in the ghettoes. It is not a matter of choice for these poor and suffering people of this nation It is like living in a sudden nightmare where hope is simply but despair. It is like a living hell, dead and alive, being buried alive in a beautiful grave with eyes wide open and with none to weep or care. It is like living like a destitute in Hollywood or Las Vegas. It is like seeing gold, diamonds and platinum, but you cannot have any of it to better your life.

While the government spends billions of dollars on military hardware, reconstruct roads, bridges, and create new structures which is not a bad thing to do, or spend billions of rand on certain programs and projects which does not empower the vast majority of individual lives personally in upgrading their living standards as proof that the government is working hard to make human infrastructures better; it is agreeable that all these billions of dollars and resources should be channelled especially towards having qualitative basic human needs for all South Africans.

In this way, they too can be part of the life in society. A lot of people are financially and socially dead, economically buried, simply waiting for their real funerals by the undertakers. Such enormous funds and taxpayers revenue can be spent directly on the people to better their lives and upgrade their human standard of living. The lives of all these millions of people can be reconstructed and reawakened, so that their dead bones can wake up, arise and shine. Homeless people can have social welfare for council housing, feeding schemes for those who cannot put food on their table for their families, incentives for clothing, medical cards and pocket money to spend until they find their feet to become fully whole again in society.

South Africans cannot have social equality in society if this is not done, and the injustice in society cannot be remedied if people remain homeless or forced to live in shacks, hopeless and helpless. Until people have the basic standard of life which includes proper furnished housing, clothing, food, medical card, and pocket money to spend pending their employment, they can never see or appreciate the beauty or development in South Africa, and the incidence of violence and crime will continue to erupt like an active volcano in society.

This is why the government must for once tackle this problem because of all its merits. People who have furnished homes will not buy stolen goods from junkies to put in their homes which already have these basic needs, and those people with homes will not wish to break into other people's homes which are like theirs, and people with basic human needs will not envy the needs of others. The first step to fighting crimes and violence is to ensure human rights and dignity of life. When there is dignity of life, people tend to maintain their human dignity and would not wish to lose it for the life in incarceration.

Guaranteeing a basic standard of living is what leads to human growth and development. Every basic human need is all and the same for everyone on earth and any responsible government that guarantees these needs for its entire people is the government of the people, by the people and for the people. This is what freedom and democracy is all about, and a government that ignores this fact is a struggling government that will struggle and continue to struggle in vain till the end of time.

Lack of this kind of government in most parts of Africa is responsible for the poverty in Africa as a third world continent full of civil strife, insecurity of lives and properties, as well as rebellion and genocide. This is why it is so sad in the African continent with all its natural and mineral resources, whose resources that lay abound on the earth are not used effectively by our leadership to guarantee Africans basic human needs. African resources are being wrongfully managed by most African leaders over the century.

Most of these African leaders have failed us as Africans and have made mockery of African freedom, independence and democracy. It is so sad that they cannot even provide us with basic human needs that fulfill the promise of African independence and democracy as it is done in Ireland.

Today as Africans, it is so unfortunate and shameful that we have no shame. Some of our shameless leaders gather themselves together without shame at their AU summits like penguins in Buckingham palace wearing European suits and traditional attires busy doing what does not fulfil our hopes and dreams. Many of them are just there to represent their corruption and greed. Many of them simply attend these summits to defend their legacies of national shame and disgrace. They are there without shame or disgrace, each one representing the failures, the suffering of their people, and reminding us daily how terribly shameful we are to have some of these people as our leaders from one government to the other.

As Africans, I enjoin that everyone should sit on the floor in shame wherever we are for at least three minutes daily, cover our heads with sack cloth and mourn for poor African leadership from one generation to the other, and observe three minutes of silence for all their failures. In this way, I believe we will see the light of hope and be able to decide objectively what future we wish for our future generations. We need the future

Nelson Mandela's ideal leadership wished for all our people and mankind. We wish our African leaders to borrow the heart and mind of Nelson Mandela in other to move Africa forward. There is no other choice, love and progress is all we need.

It is unimaginable for example that a country that sells millions of barrels of crude oil daily cannot provide basic human needs for all its people, and worse still, the people who own the land from which the crude oil is being produced and processed are the poorest in the world today. Their land and farms are polluted and degraded, and remains the most underdeveloped in human history in oil producing regions of the world. This is the dilemma in Niger Delta states in Nigeria, a typical example of African failures of our hopes and dreams. What a terrible example of shame and disgrace in the heart of corruption and greed? Despite all these, our people in that nation are the most boastful and arrogant people in the African continent who think they are very clever, smart, intelligent and are the giant of Africa. Being a giant does not mean the giant of corruption and greed, but to strive and become the giant of goodwill, peace and progress. We do not want to become the giant of Boko Haram and acts of terrorism, corruption and greed.

If South Africa has the crude oil and natural gas that some African nations have, I believe South Africa will be greater than Europe and America, and everyone in Africa will migrate to South Africa in search of better life, same way they emigrated to Europe and America. Even without crude oil, most Africans have already migrated and occupied South Africa as if it was their own country.

South Africa is the Europe of Africa because it is still a country that is doing its best like none other in Africa to make a great difference in the lives of its people. This is the more reason why South Africa must continue to set the pace in African leadership and help teach our other African leaders the part to responsible leadership. South African leaders should not and must never follow the Nigerian style of leadership where corruption and human greed reign supreme. This advice also applies to my brothers and sisters in Nigeria who are determined to make a great difference in the lives of my people. They should become pace-setters and show Nigerians that there is hope for a greater tomorrow for all Nigerians.

One way of becoming better South Africans is through political participation. We can do this through political participation of every colour and race united together as one in the political future of this country. Majority rule does not imply majority of colour or race. It does not mean majority black, majority coloured, or majority Indians or whites. It simply means majority wins the vote. Forming a majority rule is not about majority colour rule or majority race rule. This is something we must understand and become part of the majority rule.

We must sneak out of our minority shells and become part of the majority rule and decide the future of this great nation. We must stop to brand ourselves into colour or race groups, or into minority groups. You will only become a minority if you make yourself a minority. It is time to belong to everyone and become part of a great national family. A family with all colours and race is the greatest rainbow family on earth. That is why the United States of America is proud of its greatness as the greatest nation on earth.

South Africa is the only hope and role model for all Africans. This is why our people need to come together as one, united and strong, and invest on qualitative basic human needs in their social welfare system and try to control its border posts with proper migration policies to enable them provide a qualitative social welfare system for all its people and productive immigrants to their land. Because there is no qualitative social welfare system to cater for automatic basic human needs, some people in South Africa are angry and frustrated. They express this anger and rage in crimes and violence, destroying the efforts of government in the so-called reconstruction process. The government must therefore place much premium on developing human lives more than the emphasis placed on the development of rocks and stones. As I may rightly say, *"An African child, who refuses to enjoy the ideal comfort of a cosy European pram, shall suffer from being tied with scarf or a towel to the aching backbones of the mother's back".*

It is therefore imperative that the pro-democracy government now in South Africa should help our brothers and sisters make the necessary decision whether to tie an African child with a scarf or towel to the back of the mother's aching backbones, or empower the father to push the child around in the shopping malls with a cosy European pram among other white folks in our land.

South Africa today is faced with a lot of challenges, which is making everyone very nervous in the society. Basic standard of living has deteriorated amidst high cost of living. Corruption and poor service delivery is said by critics to be hampering the efforts of its people to have a better life. Even so, there is not much corruption in South Africa compared to other African nations; hence there is the urgent need in not allowing this aspect of social ill to be part of government hidden agenda. There is need for accountability in government and the necessity to prosecute corrupt cases without let or failure.

This is because we all know how corruption has dragged the African continent to its knees. This experience is visible in Nigeria, Egypt, Tunisia, Zimbabwe, Angola, Kenya, Cameroon, Swaziland, Democratic Republic of Congo, and most other parts of the African continent. The South African currency, which is the Rand, is no longer as strong as it use to be during the apartheid era, or even in 1994, while Botswana a small neighbouring country still have a very strong currency far better than that of South Africa, even though this small country depends on South Africa for most goods and services.

The racial divide, poverty, crime and violence are deepening in society amidst frustrations and struggle to survive in the community. Inflation of goods and services is eating deep into the pockets of its citizens, while low wages and the high rate of unemployment are inflaming the tensions in society. Despite all these problems, South Africa is a wonderful country distinct from all other African nations in every possible way and by every means in its complex nature and historical perspective. It is like a diamond twinkling like a star.

In truth, South Africa is the most beautiful country on earth in terms of its cultural heritage, nature reserve, and the beauty of the landscapes amidst development efforts. It is like saying that black is proud. Everything about South Africa is purely South African, something that cannot and will never be seen anywhere on earth. As a country which is like a diamond twinkling like a star, the good life in this country is only limited to very few people, who are privileged in society. There is no basic standard of living for the vast majority of the people, and not many people may ever find their stars shinning in this country.

While many people are happy with good life and shinning stars, other stars are bleak and dark if hope is not lifted up in the lives of these people to shine better. It is very difficult for most people to understand what is happening in this country or believe that all fingers are not equal. The conditions of life of anyone in South Africa forms individual opinion about life in this country. Even harder is the difficulty of some leaders to understand what other people are going through in this country because they are not in the situation of other people.

As former President Thabo Mbeki would rightly say, *"We live in two worlds in South Africa"*. These two worlds are sub-divided into individual worlds, each individual world not understanding the world of each other. This is the irony of life in this country where public opinion is inconclusive about South Africa. In understanding the world of other races, especially the white race, Nelson Mandela decided to learn the Afrikaans language in his Robben Island prison jail, and made friendship with his enemies. He did this as a wonderful leader with a great foresight, so that he could understand the secret of the white man's success, and share this success with all his people.

However, as an African country being ruled by a black man, all that twinkles are no stars, and all that glitters is no gold. This is what usually happens when a country is being ruled by black people; there is loss of confidence and self esteem. Investors starve the government of investment opportunities and foreign investors lack the confidence to invest their funds without reservations. There is a plot and conspiracy by the world global market to deliberately devalue the currency and frustrate black governments from moving a step ahead of the times. This kind of blackmail by the countries of the West is the problem the government is facing in South Africa. Though today, they smile at South Africa and regard the country as trading partners and friend, they are not very happy that South Africa has gained its freedom and democracy.

They wish the white people were still in power and authority so that they could become better partners as brothers of the same sword. This is the hypocrisy that exists on earth. Even China comes in styles like a monkey seeking for banana; knowing that Africa have no choice but to fall for such trades and products we cannot refuse. It is like saying that a monkey cannot refuse banana. We want good things of life without making the necessary sacrifices of producing these goods and services for all our people. We need cheap Chinese goods and services same way monkeys need banana. We should learn to compete with China as trade partners and in the manufacturing industry, in science and technology. We must not allow China to colonize us with their goods and services.

That is why China has seized that opportunity to help us where we cannot help ourselves. This is the genesis of the Chinese policy in Africa. They come to help us with loans, goods and services, and at the same time they pay their people back home to devise ways and means to collect back their money from us a thousand times over through trade, goods and services.

They pay and encourage their people to come to Africa and reap our economy bare of all monies from these goods and services. They become richer and live better life, create more employment for their teeming population, raise their gross domestic growth index, and become more industrialized, while we become poorer, enslaved, corrupt, unemployed, and economically confused in the land of our ancestors.

However, we are not ungrateful to China for their cheap goods and services because we have no better choice or options. They have helped us a great deal with scientific and technological advancement, and with their cheap good and services. Half bread is better for Africans than nothing. Even cheap unhealthy food is better than hunger and starvation. It is better to die of cheap unhealthy food, than to die of Ebola fever.

Imagine Britain creating a sculptural piece of Nelson Mandela in London in honour of former President Nelson Mandela and made it a Park in Britain for tourists because they knew and appreciated the Mandela legacies, his sterling qualities as the greatest leader of our time. They did this because they knew what was good for all humanity. They knew that Mandela was an Icon.

While Britain recognized Mandela as an honest and great leader, some of our African leaders were very jealous of him. Robert Mugabe once described Mandela as a prisoner with only prison experience and prison ideas of leadership. He bluntly said he did not need any advice from Mandela on how to rule his country Zimbabwe. That explains the state of mind of most poor and greedy African leadership which does not recognize anything good in human lives.

It is a very good thing that the world and Britain recognized a man they once classified and called a terrorist. At the same time, they awarded this great man a Nobel Peace Prize he shared with former President Frederick De Klerk of the former apartheid regime. This is the case of a former colonial master and sponsor of apartheid regime honouring those who fought against them and took away their colonial powers from their apartheid and colonial government. Is this a genuine honour or honour of hypocrisy? Despite this ambiguity of life, the irony of fate, Britain showed love to a man who was caught in a circle of irony in life. It was a circle of love and hate in human existence.

However, South Africans and the world are very grateful to the British government and appreciate all their efforts both in the past and present as members of the Commonwealth of Nations. There is a lot of historical links between the United Kingdom and South Africa, which includes people with ancestral background. Back in South Africa, in the midst of happiness there is always danger of crime, violence, insecurity of life and properties. It is this danger that looms over the heads of all those who are happy and fulfilled in their accomplishments in this country. Those mostly in danger are those who have investments, properties and something to lose. These include those who are successful, the white people, the educated and skilled black South Africans, and the successful coloured people in society who live daily in fear for their lives.

South Africa is not a fearful nation, and bearing this in mind, it is a good thing that everyone in this nation must unite together to face up to this demon of crime and violence. The incidence of crime and violence in society is not only the problem of government to tackle, but the problem of all South Africans, something that needs the cooperation of every community to combat and rid the society of this menace.

Blaming the government will not help anyone because the police cannot control the thoughts of people, or enter into their minds and diagnose their intents. The behaviour and character of people in our various communities will give us as individuals insights into reporting suspicious characters to the police for monitoring their activities before they strike at us and our children.

The community is responsible for every crime committed in any community and not the government. The community must blame itself for any crime committed in that community and do something to rid its community of such crimes and violence against its community. It is as simple as that because these criminal elements are members of the community and we know who they are in the community. This is what people in Britain do.

It is very difficult for the police to act effectively in their fight against crime without community forums and help to bring criminals to justice. There is little the police can do and there is much the community can do in the fight against crime in South Africa. We must accept this fact and face up to it if we wish to live in safety and security of lives and properties in our various communities in this country.

By fighting crimes and violence in our various communities, we have done our part in community policing to rid South Africa of crime and violence for the common good of society, investors, foreign investors, businesses, and the tourism and hospitality industry which would bring in the investment and capital needed by government and everyone for national growth and development. This will help to create employment opportunities and go a long way to help the government acquire the capital necessary for qualitative social welfare benefits required to ensure all South Africans basic human needs and restoration of human dignity in our hopes and dreams.

We must all stop this grave evil and danger of crime and violence in society and treat it as an evil greater than that of the apartheid regime. It is greater and worse than the apartheid regime because it is a threat to the existence of all South Africans irrespective of colour or race or social background or status. It is a threat to humanity as acts of terror. Criminals must be treated as terrorists because they are terrorizing the lives of everyone in the communities. The 'People Against Gangterism and Drugs', PAGAD tried to set the pace in the fight against organized crime and drugs, but unfortunately they took the laws into their hands in Cape Town in their fight in the positive affirmative to rid their communities of crime and violence.

Unfortunately, while their intentions was genuine, there were some members of that organization whose intentions were deep rooted in hidden agendas, overt unkindness and envy. Some of these members were themselves hardened criminals, jailbirds, murderers and gangsters. All these factors worked against the group and worse still, they acted in the wrong way by taking the laws into their hands in a jungle justice system. PAGAD must help to set a pace in community development and energize the various communities in South Africa to awaken to the task of nation building within the due process of the law. Communities must be seen to have greater ties as grass-root in the soul of the business of the state.

Communities must be stronger than all the three tiers of government in other to help create a balance between the good, the bad and ugly situations in South Africa. People must not take the laws into their hands in this process.

This is not acceptable, immoral, against the constitution and human rights. Even so, PAGAD have tried to make a great difference in the fight against crime. They were not perfect, but at least they tried to do something. Doing something is what is important, but it must be done within the due process of the law. The law is supreme, and things must be done accordingly in other not to create jungle justice system and destabilize the very institution we try to protect its interest.

It is this same danger of crime and violence that took away the life of South African famous musician, Lucky Dube, and many other South Africans who were the breadwinners in their families and shinning stars in the land. This grave danger in society is not only the danger of crime and violence, but the danger of drugs and alcohol abuse which is like knocking on the devil's door. It is so sad and unfortunate that our dear lovely sister of the blessed memory, one of the greatest musicians of our time, and a young artist with a great future ahead of her, Brenda Fasi got caught up in the circle of alcohol and drugs abuse which took her away from us unceremoniously.

Today, we miss all the people or souls of the faithful departed who got snatched away from us through the circle of crime, violence and drugs abuse in our society, knowing that though they are gone, they will never be forgotten, and their memories lay buried at the depth of our hearts and minds. Though they are gone, we owe them all a duty to fight for them, and continue to fight against those forces and factors in society which took away their lives.

They deserve your fight. Innocent children, babies and women who were raped, killed and mutilated, deserve your fight. Our mothers and grandmothers who were raped, robbed, or killed deserve your fight. Our innocent brothers and sisters who were hurt or killed in every family in South Africa by criminals deserve your fight. This nation deserves your fight. All those innocent people who died and sacrificed their lives during the days of apartheid regime to free this country and give us true freedom and democracy which we enjoy today deserve your fight. The founding fathers of freedom and democracy deserve your fight. We cannot and must not allow this evil of crime and violence in society to prevail and defeat us.

"SAY NO TO CRIME!" Rise up in a million marches in all your various communities without taking the laws into your hands and "SAY NO TO CRIME!" The future generations of this great country and innocent babies yet unborn deserve your fight until that day, when a criminal is seen and regarded as a fugitive with nowhere to run and nowhere to hide. This is the fight! A fight against enemies of the state is a national cause. A fight against enemies of the people is a fight against terrorism.

In this fight, describing South Africa as a diamond twinkling like a star is like digging into the depth of the earth for gold in that country, which has to go through a furnace to regain its beauty in other to determine its carats. It is like uncut diamonds and gemstones in Kimberly, which needed serious polishing and cut into aesthetic geometric shapes in other to appreciate its beauty, its purity, and its clarity.

By fighting the incidence of crimes and violence in society, the beauty and radiance, the good life we seek in our hopes and dreams will be established with time in our lives. The beauty and clarity of South Africa will start to manifest itself for all to see. The diamond in us will make us shine like the stars in our lives.

This battle against crime and violence is the first step to realization, national growth and development, as well as peace, truth, and reconciliation. The government needs help from the people, and the people also need help from the government. This unity is very necessary to bring about the fulfilment of our hopes and dreams in society. Such is the irony of the present conditions of life in a place where people need help in other to decide their own destiny.

Until our people are united as one with the government and help the government in whichever way we can, there is no credible system to solve all the current problems in society. It is currently like a system that has no purity or clarity in which way the future is heading to for the vast majority of the people. To many people, there is hope, and for a lot of people the future is very tense and bleak, not knowing which road to follow.

Joe Odiboh

Chapter 3
No More Tears

Whichever way the future is heading to; whichever road is there to follow; South Africans will weep no-more. It is time to arise and shine above our problems and tackle the three worse enemies in our national life. These enemies are poverty, crime and violence, and racial bias. If we attack these problems in our new found struggle to free ourselves from these three monsters, it will bring us dignity of life and respect for one another as one people in one nation. These are the three primary problems in this country.

We all know that most people are poor and impoverished which also lead to the high rate of crime in society. We know that no amount or population of visible policing can stop the crimes in this nation. The solution is to tackle individual problem of poverty and lack of human dignity. People need to have human dignity and a sense of belonging and better life for all for the society to become more pleasurable and productive. A very good social welfare system that provides every individual with a good home, feeding, clothing and basic human needs is the answer to human dignity for life to become meaningful for the people.

A careless walk within an impoverish community, both in the black and coloured communities will expose you to the real danger in society, and how dangerous a careless walk could be in such a free and democratic society. It could become, "The walk of death". The way forward is the fight against crime and violence in our various communities in other to end the tears in our eyes.

That is the way forward because if a child or someone cannot move around freely in the community without being robbed, raped or killed, there is no way forward. The government is already doing its work to move the country forward for the various communities, but crime and violence is hampering this effort, and the way forward is not the "Walk of Death".

There are other people in the world today whose only impression of South Africa is the incidence of reported crimes and violence on television screens and the pictures of our people's living conditions in informal settlement or poor communities. These pictures and impressions are the handiwork of the third force in our society who is determined to paint the picture of South Africa in a terrible and miserable image. These are some of the images the South African government is trying desperately to erase by the provision of RDP housing programs and projects, and through black empowerment affirmative action's of government.

There are so many other people in the world who wonders what makes South Africa so special and different from the rest of the African continent, and why its historical perspective makes it like a country founded on top of an active volcano? Strangers will wonder, what it is about South Africa that tingle the ears, and make the heart beat like the uncontrollable flicker of the eyelids?

The answers to such questions are very obvious with its plethora of national problems, so complex, so difficult to resolve, and so fragile that if not handled and solved in very special and complex ways and means, the active volcano might erupt into uncontrollable crises situation, especially as leadership continue to change hands in the ANC and other political parties, and as the trust or confidence people have in their leaders starts to fade into the mist.

It is true that the country became more united than ever before and had great hopes and dreams during the reign of late former President Nelson Mandela. As leadership shifted hands from this great legend to former President Thabo Mbeki, and then moved to President Jacob G Zuma, the trust between the people and the government began to diminish slowly but surely. And now that Nelson Mandela is gone, this anxiety will grow even stronger as the years go on in our passage of life.

Lack of confidence did not diminish because of President Jacob Zuma, but because human wants and needs are starting to go higher than expected and the people are beginning to lose their patience. While so many people have been positively empowered with better conditions of life, and have received RDP housing programs, education and gainful employment, there are others who are still in the waiting list, frustrated and loss of perseverance.

Many of these people are the ones who are always seen protesting and destroying government infrastructures and frustrating the efforts of government with their frustrations which in turn is not a way forward. Most protest marches in South Africa are carried out by black or coloured people and not the white people. The way forward is not through violent protests or destruction of infrastructures and government programs and projects. Rome was not built in a single day same way that good things do not come easy. There is need for understanding and appreciation in other to move forward. The fact is that the government is doing something and have programs and policies in place which is moving the country forward in the right direction. This is something that needs to boost the morale of the people.

As the morale of these people starts to run low from one leadership to the other, there is beginning to be that fear of the unknown, especially after President Jacob Zuma's tenure of office is long finished, and long after that period. This fear of the unknown and certain people feeling larger than the government or above the law, and the multiplicity of the general feeling of the people is like a ticking time bomb, an earthquake brewing in the air for no apparent reasons.

One way of making the political system stronger, is to have a national party that embraces people of every race, colour and creed. There is need for two political parties as it is in the United States. The ANC can be transformed to South African National Congress, SANC to embrace every one of every race and colour, governed on merit and not on the colour of the skin. It should be transformed as a new party with new hopes and dreams for all South Africans.

It should be a political party where even the white or coloured man or woman can be elected on merit as the party leader or to head the government on merit not on the basis of colour, and with the full support of everyone in the party. If President Barrack Obama can be elected by the Democrats to lead and rule in America, the ANC, or SANC can do better for the common good of all South Africans.

It is time to think forward and forget about a party founded on the principles of freedom and struggles. South Africa needs a new political order that embraces everyone of every race joining together as one in the same party to decide the future of South Africa. This is the way forward in South Africa political spectrum. Even so, South Africans are great people, patient and very tolerant people who know that South Africa is above anyone, or any single individual, community or race. Yet, it is important to move a step ahead of the time now by working together to try and take stock of the destiny of this great nation.

How we do this is a question of principles and moral discipline. It is therefore advisable that this period of patience should be used for positive thinking and creative ideas knowing that if you think like a millionaire, your hopes and dreams to become a millionaire will manifest itself in your life as long as you put your creative ideas into full practice and hard work.

These are decisions people need to make as alternative to violent acts and crimes. It is unhealthy for people to do nothing about their lives and simply wait for the government to do everything for them. People must not wait for things to fall apart in their lives before doing the little they can to better their lives. The difference between man and animals is that man is a rational being with a purpose and mission in life. Man is not a product of hopelessness and emptiness. Man cannot just wonder around on earth, robbing people, killing, raping, and remain unproductive. Man must work.

People must stop the culture of helplessness and hopelessness in society, because hopelessness and emptiness is a personal choice for those who have nothing good to offer mankind. In the same way, poverty is a personal and national choice. According to Nelson Mandela, "I am the captain of my own ship. I am the master of my soul" We must feel challenged enough to be captains of our ship, and masters of our fate. Those people who have nothing to offer mankind cannot offer anything to themselves or to their families and communities.

We must understand that there are people in life who have sacrificed their lives and worked day and night not for themselves or their families but to better the living conditions on earth. This is a matter of human sacrifice, the same way Mandela sacrificed his life to set us free.

People ventured into the moon, and sent robots to Mars. People created satellites and satellite networks. People found solutions to certain illness that consumed mankind. People belong to different trades and professions. People have sacrificed so much to raise our standard of living and created things in science and technology to make the world a better place. What then are we as individuals doing in South Africa to make the world a better place to live?

Our people must borrow leafs from these great people and think of what we can do for humanity and not in what humanity can do for us. Whatever humanity does for us, man must live and die. But whatever man does for humanity becomes a long and lasting legacy that never dies.

We must learn as South Africans to believe in ourselves. We must believe that we can fly and touch the sky. We must believe that we can be united together as one and make South Africa the best place to live on earth. We must believe that the sacrifices and bloodshed in the past is a pole vault to greater heights and achievements in life. We must not forget that the first world heart transplant was done in South Africa. This should remind us of the great potentials that lay as virgins in us.

If as a man, we think and do things like progressives, and keep this hope alive while doing the right things in life, the propensity or chances of becoming a progressive nation draws even nearer. Hope and hard work, dedication to a cause, and the ability to keep on trying each time we fail is the key to success in life.

Success in life is not success in the sense of the word. It is about how much efforts one has put into life to achieve success. It is the ability to keep hope alive in the pursuance of certain aims and goals in life. Celebration of success is a celebration of human efforts in life to make ends meet. We cannot say that because we are poor, we must eat from the rubbish dumps. We can learn and try to grow our own crops, and practice organic farming system behind our backyards, or in wasted lands and street corners.

Whether we fail or succeed in life is not entirely the story of success or failures in life. It is the story of how much we rise up to face our challenges each time we fell. Nelson Mandela fell a thousand times in his commitment to freedom and democracy in South Africa. He and many others were beaten, battered, crucified, incarcerated and brutalized. They never gave up hope and never stopped fighting for that which they believed in, "The Freedom Chapter".

They remained steadfast to their cause and never gave up hope or became selfish. They were believers in freedom and democracy for all. They suffered and waited decades after decades, hoping and waiting and believing that tomorrow will bring a better day for all South Africans. In the midst of destruction and deaths, they were prepared to die for their cause. They were resilient and were fighters. They were captains of their ship. They were masters of their craft.

They were masters of their fate. This is the story of success in South Africa, something that cannot be easily found in all other parts of the African continent. We cannot think of success if we are corrupt. It is in Nigeria we know that people celebrate their success in life in measure of corruption. Nigerians celebrate most corrupt people because of the enormous wealth they have and what they own as individuals. People are honoured in that country by what they own and not by what they are as individuals. This is why everyone is encouraged to become corrupt in public office, in civil service, industry and enterprise. This is why corruption has become the bedrock of a system that is dysfunctional.

Those who are not privileged to be part of this system have developed their own system of fraudulent means and practices, 419, armed robbery, and kidnapping of innocent progressive Nigerians. This is what happens in a culture of corruption and greed in a nation. As Nigerians, the leadership and sterling qualities of late former President Nelson Mandela, and his life is a handwriting in the walls of our life. His humility, kindness, and simplicity are virtues we must teach to our future generations. It must be taught in schools that humility is the soul of business and nation building.

We must celebrate the life of Mr. Mandela by complete and total change in our character and general conducts, attitude, beliefs, and the culture of corruption and greed in our society. Let us be seen as humane people and not as arrogant thieves, suicide bombers and kidnappers. Let us be seen as people committed to the welfare of Nigeria and not to the welfare of our wallets and bank accounts. Let us be seen as candid honest people and not as liars and fraudsters.

There are too many people in Nigeria who have sacrificed their lives and are doing so much to make Nigeria great. Let us join with these progressives. Let us identify the good and honourable people in our society and honour them as people with respect and dignity. Let us stop hailing and clapping after corrupt people and fraudsters and show them the part of truth, honour and sincerity of purpose in life.

Let us use the crude oil income to ensure universal free education for all Nigerians, and establish the most viable social welfare system that brings better life for all to all Nigerians and all those yet unborn. This will ultimately end the circle of corruption and greed, frauds, kidnapping, and the acts of terrorism in this great nation. In this way, no one will envy other people or encourage sycophants in society.

A better life for all in Nigeria means a better house for all, better educational system and institutions, better health and medical services, better infrastructural facilities, mechanized farming and cooperative farming and enterprise, regular hygienic water supply, 24 hrs power supply, and ensuring for all Nigerians the basic human needs that fulfils the promise of true Nigerian independence.

There should be public accountability to the people, a just and fair judicial system devoid of fraudulent practices and favouritism, and a police system that is not corrupt and answerable to the people. Nigeria needs to be run not by individuals but by a functional system that caters for the needs of society. It is not about one regime change after the other, but about functionality of a system that works for the good of society. Nigerians have never witnessed or experienced such a system in their lives. Those Nigerians abroad and all over the universe, and all those who have travelled out of Nigeria can help Nigerians establish such a system. This is the only partway to Nigerian problems and woes.

Where there is corruption, nothing works in the right way. There is no guarantee of fundamental human rights. There is no social justice for anyone except those who have corruptly enriched themselves. There is abuse of power and compromise in official duties. The police and judicial system suffers because they become the curators of corruption and human greed. Corruption eats deep like a cancer into the moral fabric of society. Hope turns to despair. At the end, we become wolves in sheep skin, and lose our moral values and principles. In search of our moral values and principles, we create more churches in our search for hope. The cancer in the society creeps like virus, a very corrupt virus and corrupts most of the churches absolutely in the name of God.

Our people spend days and night praying instead of creating ideas on how to make Nigeria a better place. We pray for food to eat instead of embarking in agricultural growth and development. We pray for money instead of creative ideas that will create jobs and enterprise like the 'Nollywood' and our music industry.

We believe more in prayers than we believe in ourselves and our ability to rise to greater heights in life. We seem to forget that it was not prayers and churches that made China and Japan industrialized nations. We seem to forget that manufacturing industries and factories were started by people at home, in their garages and empty spaces. In Nigeria we use every empty space and our houses for church premises because of the benefits we hope to derive from it in the name of God.

Germany did not pray for industrial revolution to take place in that country. The civilized world was not built upon the foundations of prayers. Unfortunately for us, all the things we pray to have and own in our corrupt nature and greed are owned by the civilized world not by their dedication to prayers but through hard work, and the choices they made for their people and future generations. China has the biggest market on earth for all products, goods and services. They did this through researches, hard work and dedication.

You do not need to go to church in Ireland to have a fully furnished flat, own as many good cars as you wish so long you pay your insurance, road tax and have your NCT, eat any kind of food you wish, and receive the best medical attention on earth, and free of charge if you have no job. It is about a functioning system and not about churches and prayers. We know that prayers are very necessary in life as a life line, but using and abusing prayers is another issue entirely. This is how we as Nigerians have abused the institutions of churches for our selfish personal interest and selfish gains. In this country, fraudsters pray for 'mugu to drop' or their victims to pay money. Others result to occults to hypnotize or influence the minds of their victims to pay money through the powers of darkness.

I believe we are using and abusing the service of God. Like Jesus Christ rightly said, "Beware of false prophets, for many of them will come in my name". There is no place on earth where many churches have sprang up and many false prophets have resurrected than Nigeria. This is what the endemic of corruption and greed can do to society. They become very wealthy churches wealthier than the state. Everyone becomes a pastor richer than the Head of the State. That is what corruption and greed can do to a very corrupt nation. That is why as Nigerians, it is time for us to use the lesson of the life of Nelson Mandela to reflect on our lives as individuals and in the life of our nation. We must learn to be content with who we are and not in what we own.

This is not the time for foolish arguments about religion and prayers. It is not about creating our own churches and becoming prophets of hope or prophets of doom. It is not about condemning any church or prophets; it is about the question of morality and conscience. It is not about the properties we own or how elegant and most respectful people adore us; it is about how we truly feel inside of us.

We have to make the right choice now either to be content with what we are or disown what we own. We can distant ourselves from what we own by using what we own for the good of society. This comes back to Jesus Christ, when he asked the rich man to give up his wealth and follow him on a missionary crusade. We all know the answer to that question. One thing is very clear that we cannot worship God and mammal at the same time. There is no pastor who wishes to live very simple or pure spiritual life devoid of wealth and properties in Nigeria today. It's all about the money through tithes and offerings or building funds.

A pastor with a private jet does not quote the Bible saying that, "it is easier for the camel to pass through the eyes of a needle than for the rich and material person to enter into the kingdom of God". Because of corruption in society, both pastors and their followers only read and preach the Bible to suit financial and social gains. Everything is done for personal interest which is selfish, unskilful, and immoral. On the last day, no pastor will fly with a private jet into the kingdom of God.

Nobody wants to live a simple life anymore. Everyone wants to be sophisticated, without truly working hard to be productive in making life more meaningful for our people.

Nobody wants to be a carpenter, a tailor, goldsmith, panel beater, spray painter, handyman, electrician, or get involved in skills development. Everyone wants to be a pastor because of the lucrative Christian trade. People pray to succeed in armed robbery, in fraudulent means and practices, and for God to give them the opportunity in life to work in places where they can be blessed in corruption. As these corrupt people become blessed in corruption, they too bless the church with their corrupt money and illegal assets.

In this way, society and the churches become blessed in corruption in our country, Nigeria. That is the source of the wealth in most churches. Here in our religious system, it is everyman for deals, and God prosper us all with Holy Ghost fire.

Whether I am condemned by mankind or not for saying all these, the truth remains that in a corrupt society, some heads of churches are far richer than the President of that nation in the name of God. As good as this may seem, like the President, they do not know or care whether their followers are hungry or have eaten before coming to the church. They do not know or care whether some of the people falling in spirit as possessed in their churches are falling from alcohol and drugs overdose, or hunger and starvation. Our leaders riding on private jets are unable to provide for their followers. Sad, isn't it? Like our leaders, their followers provide jets and jetties for them. Blessed isn't it? Good! To God is the glory.

However, it is never too late to mend the seriously broken fences in the kingdom of God where Mandela now lives and dwell. While we still have time, let's make amends. It is time for sober reflections in our lives. The onus rest on us as Nigerians and as a nation to decide what role or part we intend to play in becoming the captain of our nation, or the masters of our destiny. The choice is ours to make Nigeria the giant of Africa with all our human, natural and mineral resources, or make it the cockroach of West Africa with our corruption and human greed. The choice rests on every single Nigerian, to decide our future. We are the masters of our fate. We are the captains of our ship.

The problems of corruption are not only in Nigeria but all over the universe. Let us not forget that corruption made late former President Mobutu to betray his own brother, Patrick Lumumba, and sold off his country the Democratic Republic of Congo to his oppressors. He plunged his country into hell and left them in tatters. That is the difference between the DRC and South Africa. While Nelson Mandela and the ANC members stood together, tall and firm, incorruptible; the Congolese people became a house divided against it-self. They did not learn any lesson from Nelson Mandela. This division in the DRC have continued to this day because a house divided against it-self shall not stand.

Mobutu became so corrupt and unpatriotic that his country had become an African shame and continental disgrace. At the end, he was pushed out by Laurent Kabila in a civil war. Mobutu died a very lonely death in exile shortly after his exit from the DRC. He died in shame and national disgrace. Laurent Kabila was not allowed to live by his enemies. He was shot and killed by his own bodyguards who betrayed him the same way Mobutu betrayed Patrick Lumumba. As the saying goes, "Those who live by the sword shall die by the sword". Joseph Kabila his son took over power from his late father.

The legacy Mobutu left behind for Laurent Kabila, Joseph Kabila and the Congolese people was the legacy of war, rebellion and genocide. It was a legacy of betrayal of trust. It was the legacy of disunity, poverty and underdevelopment in the DRC. The only good thing Mobutu encouraged his people to do during his decades in office and left behind for them, was the legacy of men and women bleaching and toning their black dark skins to look lighter with cosmetics. He taught them the culture of moral laxity, laziness and how men must tone their skins to look like the French people. He taught them these skin tone process because his government was a cosmetic administration meant to blindfold his own people.

The time he and his people would have used in the development of the DRC and nation building, was spent by their men in painting their faces and lips. They fell in love with Paris, another man's nation and the long pants and designers collections, and they completely forgot that their country needed national growth and development.

They were content with music, drama, dance, beer and white wine from Paris. Every day for them was like Christmas. Shake....shake. Groove...groovy. They completely lost track of time and the development needs of their country. They completely forgot about their own destiny, shook their ass, twisted their waist, and danced away their lives.

There was complete lack of foresight in the society. Nobody ever dreamt of what tomorrow could bring. It was like a lost generation without a foresight or future ambitions, until Laurent Kabila awakened the people back to consciousness and realization. He did it with brutal force and loss of lives.

When Mobutu was finally dethroned and the people woke up to realization, they just stayed there and stared into the distant future. They were confused because they did not know what they wanted, or how to go about it. They did not know anything about freedom and democracy because they have never seen one. They did not know anything about collective responsibility or governance because Mobutu was a dictator.

They did not know anything about government programs or agendas and how a system works. There were no infrastructural facilities, roads or any form of developmental programs or agendas because Modutu treated the country and everyone like his own personal property. It was a dead system with a dead leader and all these confused everyone and the soldiers. The bodyguards did not understand why they overthrew and killed their leader, because there was nothing to show for it by Laurent Kabila.

The guards in their ignorance thought the only way to see the difference between Mobutu and Laurent Kabila regime was to use the only language and means they understood; the gun. They thought killing Kabila also will make a great difference or make the country to be developed overnight. They shot and killed Laurent Kabila and the situation grew worse. Then, they felt that the solutions to the Congolese problems were to keep killing their leaders one by one. They targeted Joseph Kabila, and when they could not get him killed, they went into another civil war. They called one of their rebel group M23.

These groups of soldiers put their personal animosity and self ego above their national interest. They thought and believed that the answer to any problem is a bullet in the head. Ask them why they need a change of government; they cannot give any positive response. Ask them what are their programs or agendas for DRC? They will all say different things and be shouting at the top of their voices. Ask them what are their hopes and dreams for the Congolese people? They will continue to stare blankly at you because their guns cannot find answers to their questions. Who is to blame? Ignorance!

All those years in power, Mobutu had taught his people how to sing and dance away their lives. He had taught his men and musicians to look like gays and lesbians and shake their waist around the community and twist their ass all over the universe like snakes in the monkey shadow.

Congolese men were honoured by how much they can shake and twist their waist and ass. That was something very unique, and we admire these dancers all over the universe for their dance styles, and the way they shake and twist their waists. *While most of their men are busy twisting and shaking their waist around dance floors all over the universe and in society, the women of Congo are the breadwinners in their families. These Congolese women are mostly the ones working so hard to provide for their families. These women are more responsible and responsive to the needs of their nation.*

Unfortunately for them, they have no voice in their country. They can only be seen working and meeting with the needs of their men, but they must not be seen speaking out their desire to make the DRC a better place for all. They are the ones being used and abused by their men and their system. The Congolese women are the only stories of success that can be written in the books of Democratic Republic of Congo. Only a few men are working hard in their struggle to survive in that country. The Congolese leadership is a nightmare for their people, and it is a place without fundamental human rights.

It is like a system that is still very crude like crude oil, and the people and the system need to be refined so that they can see the light of hope to a better tomorrow. All the years since their independence were nothing but wasted years. It is a country that needs to start all over again from the beginning in other to have a future. Worse still, Mobutu did not leave behind the legacy of hard work, human dignity for his men and the need for social, political, economic, and technological advancement. He left behind the culture of laziness, songs and dances, sex and soul, and how to shake their waist and twist their ass on the dance floor.

In the midst of their laziness, songs and dances, most Congolese men and women have turned to the use of guns, arms and ammunitions to kill one another, rape and kill their women and children. Each party is fighting to inherit the legacy and culture of corruption in that country. The Democratic Republic of Congo is one of the richest country in

Africa, yet is one of the poorest and least developed with very poor standard of living. This was made possible because former late President Mobutu totally neglected his people and became a ceremonial president who thought he was the god of DRC. This total neglect lasted from the time of their gaining independence to the present day.

However, President Joseph Kabila is a very young man who inherited turbulent times from his assassinated father, and he has been battling to curtail the uprising in that nation. However hard this young leader may have tried to create a democratic order, there are many lessons for him to learn from the life of former late President Nelson Mandela. He needs to learn to love his own people and create an enabling circumstance for unity, peace, truth and reconciliation among the warring factions and different tribes and races in his country.

Joseph Kabila is faced with the task of creating a government of national unity where everyone can take part in the business of nation building. He must learn from Madiba how to forgive and put the past behind in their search for hope and nation building. The task of nation building and reconciliation should be uppermost in his national agenda. He must teach his people that there is dignity in labour and the need to fold up their sleeves and put the culture of fighting and dancing aside for greater tasks of nation building which is ahead for the people. He must remind his people that he alone cannot build the DRC but with the full cooperation of every Congolese people both home and abroad.

He must learn from Mandela how to forgive and release all political and military prisoners and involve everyone to channel their energy to the task of nation building.

He must call for the return back home of all Congolese people abroad to come and help and contribute by using the resources of the state for national peace and stability and to further create programs and agendas that fulfils the hopes and aspirations of the people.

This is not the time to be thinking of political victimization, or who killed whom, and who is related to Ruanda, or who is a Tutsi or a Hutu? There is more than enough work for everyone to do back home and great tasks ahead for the people to get involved in the building of a great nation for all their people.

There is enough mineral and natural resources that lay in waste in that nation, and it is enough for the people of DRC to channel towards the realization of their hopes and dreams. The abundance of land and rain forests which lay in waste must be used for mechanized agriculture and the development of agro allied industries that can feed the entire African continent.

The people of the DRC must use the celebration of the life of former President Nelson Mandela to embark on a very long walk to freedom and democracy in that country. It must be the long walk to social, political, economic, educational and technological growth and advancement. They must learn to speak English language and try to be part of the global economy and family. They must forget about the French colonial policy of assimilation and strive to be Congolese with the development of Congolese goods and services. They must learn to be proud of their fatherland.

If need be that some of the people wish to become dancers and keep the culture of music, let them do this responsibly in a way that it will enrich the lives of the people and bring about tourism, art and culture. It should be made a part of national agenda to bring in the growth and development necessary to empower the people for a better tomorrow.

Joseph Kabila must abhor the legacy of emptiness and the culture of corruption which Mobutu left behind as a legacy. Joseph can twist things around as a young man from the new generation and make the necessary 'Madiba' sacrifices necessary to turnaround the fortunes of his fatherland. Joseph must not allow the blood of his father, Laurent Kabila which he shared to set his people free go down the drain. It must not be shed in vain.

It is now time for Joseph Kabila to learn how to smile and embrace his enemies and bring them closer to himself. He must study and understand the ways of his people, what their needs are, and what is their hopes and dreams. He has every opportunity in the world right now to make history and stamp his name in the book of human kindness and goodwill to all his people. The time is now. Right now!

Joseph Kabila must embark on this long journey right now because one does not fix appointment with fate. Tomorrow will be too late, the time is now! The part will not be smooth, and the road will be rugged full of swamps, slopes, hills and mountains. He must be determined to climb the tallest mountain to bring to his people the goodies that fulfils the promise of independence.

Joseph must be resolute and determined that if need be that he dies in the process of trying to do his utmost best for the common good of all his people, let it be a cause for which he must be prepared to die. Death is inevitable, and man dies only but once.

According to Nelson Mandela, "I have fought against black domination. I have forced against white domination. I have fought against the domination of one race or colour by another. I have fought for a free and democratic South Africa where everyone is equal without regards to race or colour, and with equal opportunities for all South Africans. It is a cause which I believe in and I will continue to fight for. If need be that I must die, it is a cause for which I am prepared to die".

Joseph must stand strong and firm in his commitment to his people. Let it be known that he died trying to do everything that is right and morally just for all his people. The time is now to imbibe the spirit of Mandiba in African leadership. The time is now for Joseph Kabila to rise up to the real challenges that face the Congolese people.

The time is now to make hay while the sun shines. Joseph Kabila can make it. The people of DRC can set aside their differences and face up to the challenges that confront their people. The Congolese people must stop fighting and killing each other over political leadership. The problem now in the DRC is not about leadership but about the genuine concern of the Congolese people to honestly commit themselves to building their fatherland.

Fighting each other like animals in the bush is a sign of weakness and failure. It shows a people who have no brains to divert their energy to community growth and development. It shows that these fighters are people who do not have love for their country. It is better to build your nation than to kill each other and destroy your country. Only fools destroy their own fatherland. By destroying your fatherland, where will you run to? 'To face the humiliation of becoming an asylum seeker, prohibited persons or illegal immigrants in other nations?'

By seeking asylum in other nations, what will you become? You will become an illegal immigrant, asylum seeker, prohibited person, and illegal alien in a land that you cannot call your own? If the people in the land or nation you run to as safe haven had killed themselves and destroyed their nation, where would you have run to? A penny is wise but a pound is foolish. A word is enough for my Congolese brothers and sisters. A word is enough for my African brothers and sisters. "Be wise".

However, going back to South Africa and its own plethora of national problems, it is a high time there is a referendum on crime and violence, the criminal justice system, political partway in the formation of only a two party system where everyone can participate without racial bias or tribalism.

This must be a kind of political system where every race can belong to any of the two political parties because the ANC was formed as a freedom party in the fight against the apartheid regime.

Apartheid is gone and over, the ANC need to be scrapped and two national parties formed to represent the people either as Democrats or Republicans. This will help eliminate the low morale in political leadership and energize general participation by all in the affairs of this great nation. This will strengthen political leadership and effective administration where leaders are elected on the basis of merit and competence rather than on racial grounds and opportunist endeavours.

All these will go a long way to facilitate national peace and stability and create investment confidence, boost the economy, and bring about real national growth and development. It has to be a referendum on the path to togetherness and love.

This country needs love, so that we can be patriotic and love this country more than our personal selfish interest, race or colour, and become one nation, one destiny and one certain fruitful future. This kind of politics is participatory politics without sidelines. This is the only political health needed for a long and lasting freedom and democracy.

It is now time for everyone of every race to come together as one in control of the destiny of this great nation. It is no-longer time for ANC for the black race in Northern Cape and Eastern Cape, or DA for the coloured and white race in the Western Cape and Pretoria. It is now time for unity in diversity, togetherness as one, togetherness and love.

This is the major solution to the way forward, the true path to peaceful coexistence and a better life for all South Africans. The beginning of wisdom is the ability to call things by their right names, and as South Africans, let us be wise. The motto of the former scrapped Cape Technikon is, "Be Wise".

I recall this motto in memory of former Cape Technikon in Cape Town which has educated a lot of people and provided the manpower needed for social economic growth and development. To those former students of this institution, South Africa needs you to make this country great and proud.

Though this institution have been scrapped and replaced with a functioning University of Technology, it will be wise to scrap existing political parties and apartheid structures and systems, and replace all of them with a functioning system that address the current needs of the people.

We as South Africans have been empowered in one way or the other by the apartheid system and the current system. Those in positions of authority today are not apparently the best leaders or the best brains in South Africa.

They are people fortunate to have played active roles in the ANC and the fight for freedom and democracy. This means that they have benefited themselves in one way or the other from the circumstance of apartheid and freedom or democracy.

They were empowered by their activities of the past to become South African leaders and policy makers or public servants today, something for which they have had their rewards. Most white people also have not only benefited from the apartheid era, they are also benefiting from the current freedom and democracy because their living conditions today in South Africa was influenced by the apartheid government.

The main issue is that there are millions of people out there who do not have these opportunities and have not benefited from any side of the street. These people deserve a free and fair system devoid of the old structures and systems where they can play active roles and become a part of national agenda.

There are millions of people in the coloured communities who are neither white nor black, not knowing where to belong, how to belong, and cannot fulfil their hopes and dreams in a system that have no open doors. I know everyone understands me very clearly, as clear as ice, and we must not pretend not to understand for the sake of arguments.

The truth which of course is relative is very plain and blunt. We know that not many people would wish to lose a system that is of benefit to them and their families. This is selfish, unskilful, unwholesome, and immoral.

Patriotism means putting the interest of the country above personal interest and selfish personal gains. On that note, we remember Nelson Mandela as a selfless loving leader who put the interest of the nation above his personal or selfish interest.

Nelson Mandela never used his money to build castles and mansions on top of the Table Mountain to live in. He never focused his attention on the acquisition of wealth like a greedy man. He was never corrupt or greedy for power. He never wished to live and die in power like his brother Robert Mugabe of Zimbabwe.

Our beloved Nelson Mandela lived in houses provided for him by society, or in a little house in isolation after separation from his beloved Winnie Mandela. Mandela gave part of his salary and income to charity and children's funds throughout the short period he stayed in office and thereafter until he passed away. He never chased away anyone from his sight, both young and old, children and babies. He was always there for everyone and with everyone in loving kindness.

While the economy is still booming, and the entrance into foreign markets and trade agreements with other nations is still thriving, Mandela knew it was very important to redress and address the problems of inequality, immorality, and injustice in the society.

We can do with a social welfare service system that brings hope and joy to the lives of all the people in this country. Social welfare system is a social issue which plays a major role in the lives of the people and should not be downplayed. All the social problems in the country today resonate from social issues and social welfare.

These social problems are dangerous and unhealthy for this nation and needed serious diagnosis in other to find long and lasting solutions to these problems. Such is the state of affairs caused by the unresolved injustice of the apartheid policy of the apartheid regime in South Africa, and which today seem difficult to amend and continue to ignore the common bonds that bind the people together as a safe and secure nation.

This issue of inequality, segregation and marginalization is not something that can easily be waved away with the magic wand of freedom and democracy. It requires the collective will of the people.

One thing is to have freedom and democracy in the country; another thing is to have equal rights and justice. Another issue is how this freedom, democracy, equal rights and justice impact meaningfully on the life of every citizen without regards to race or colour. Are all the people actually equal and justified with same living conditions of life?

Are things what people hoped and dreamed about freedom and democracy? We all know these things and answers to all our questions if we don't reason like selfish and wicked people who must stop to pretend that all is well, free and fair.

The greatest injustice a man can do to himself is self-deceit. We must stop to deceive ourselves and learn to call a spade a spade so that the spade can be used rightly in the work of gardening.

The situation in South Africa is like the saying goes that, "Lets come together; does not mean, lets' join together". South Africans have come together as a nation, but it has not joined together as a people in every way and by every means. It is one country with two destinies, or two worlds flowing side by side in irony. It is a country divided against it-self socially, economically, and politically.

A lot have been done to try and resolve all these problems of injustice in the face of provocation; but however hard the government and some people have tried, no matter how much tolerance have taken root, and in whichever way the country have moved forward; the active volcano gets hotter by the day, spilling smoke into the thin air, threatening to tear the country apart.

Arch Bishop Desmond Tutu have kept on warning South Africans against the dangers of poor leadership, crime, violence and incidents of poverty in society. All his pleas for the need of a better South Africa keep on falling on deaf ears.

Things are falling apart, slowly but surely unless there is unity in diversity. The government cannot force people to be friends or to love one another. The government cannot force black people to embrace the white people or the coloured communities to embrace the Indians, or force the immigrants to unite together with the Chinese. This is a task for individuals and communities to do as a measure of togetherness and love. Even in a family, togetherness is not by force. Love is not by force in relationships.

The United States of America like South Africa was once a country divided against itself in various ways and means despite the freedom and democracy in that nation. We all know the roles of human rights activists in that nation, and the roles such people like Martin Luther King Jr. played in fighting for the rights of the black people in that nation.

The only difference between the USA and South Africa is that while the USA is predominantly of the white race, South Africa is an African country with black people as the dominant race. Here in South Africa, Africans have to fight for their human rights in their own land where there was a white minority government in the past.

This is the danger and what makes the situation complex and very dicey. Despite having their freedom and human rights, better life is lacking where the Indians and the white people are having better life than the majority of the black people. Yet, there is a black majority rule, a government of the people, which is unable to create a balance between white and black.

Creating a balance is a matter of opportunity cost, and the cost of creating this balance is very high and will take a very long time to bridge this gap except the government is able to create a vibrant, active, responsible and qualitative social welfare scheme or system that will address the basic human needs of the people. This is the only easy way out, the only solution needed to mend this gap between races and colours and bring about social equality and justice.

In a truly democratic and free South Africa, like it is in America in the election of President Barrack Obama as the 44th President of the United States, a time is sure to come when white or coloured people will be elected on merit by all South Africans to lead the country in the right direction without regards to colour or race. This is a dream that is sure to come as the people become more united as one people in one country with one destiny.

This will be a very difficult task if the ANC is not scrapped as a freedom party and if a national referendum is not carried out to reflect the will of the people to meet with the present needs, hopes and dreams.

Most South Africans are becoming tired of existing situation and circumstance; they need radical change, and are tired of old stories, old systems and structures. As the old stories and systems are passing and fading away, the new generation of South Africans are silently yearning for new opportunities, new hopes and aspirations, and a new way forward.

This is possible if there is true integration process and when people start to put the country first, rather than their colour or race. This is the dynamics of unity in diversity. Until this kind of situation of merit and patriotism takes root in South Africa, and the people start to place the country first above all other things, the country is far from the part to peace and progress.

Everyone knows that this country is still far from true freedom and democracy, and the people have been very patient and understanding. The onus rest on the government to harness this understanding and patience of the people in creating those needs and services to reassure the people that there is hope for the common man in that society. It is not fair for people to inherit the old social welfare system, old political order, or old attitude and beliefs.

Restructuring the system by doing away with old systems and structures is necessary to meet with changing situation and the current needs of the people. All these are part of service delivery systems and structures.

This issue of government service delivery is very important in society, because the people depend on the government to steer the country on the right part to peace, progress, human growth and development in shaping the course of history.

People can easily forget the past if the present situation is worth appreciating and addresses all their fears, problems, and their hopes and dreams. Addressing the present needs requires open doors, human dignity to make choices and have alternatives, opportunity costs, and a social welfare system that stand as the bedrock for human growth and development.

A good and qualitative effective social welfare system is the only aspect of government program that guarantee every citizen equal rights and justice as entrenched in the constitution.

It is the only effective instrument or government department that caters for basic human needs, the only establishment that ensures that people are not homeless, have a plate of food on their table, have clothes to wear, and have some money in the pocket for miscellaneous expenses.

Any government that is able to do this is a very successful government and will continue to succeed. Some leaders do not know this; instead they are struggling to govern with wrong advisers, wrong policies, wrong programs and projects, wrong legislation that does not address basic human needs.

After decades and decades in government, the situation remains the same or worse than ever before. It is like clearing away weeds from the farm through dedication and hard labour, only for the weeds to grow and overtake the farm after a few days, weeks or months and back to square zero in continuous waste of government funds and resources.

After some time, that farmland becomes barren as if it has never produced anything or food. This is the business of a government without qualitative and efficient social welfare system and structures to cater for basic human needs in society. It is like a hopeless and helpless business of people busy doing nothing.

It is like recycling poverty and hopelessness in society. Any government that wishes to succeed must stamp its name in history and do something great and spectacular by the nature of a vibrant and active social welfare system reforms, so that it can leave behind a long and lasting legacy for the people.

The people of South Africa and all those who fought and died to secure freedom and democracy deserve this service for their people. The newborn children lying in the incubators at Groote Schuur Hospital, or Mowbray Maternity Hospital, deserve this service.

All those suffering masses of South Africa, the silent voices, the weak and the poor, and all those millions of people who are homeless, and homeless kids on the street of Johannesburg and Cape Town deserve this service.

All those people who lay sick on the hospital beds of Somerset Hospital in Waterfront and the Tygerberg Hospital, not knowing what future there is for the families they are afraid to leave behind, deserve this service.

South Africans who honour and reverend former President Nelson Mandela as the great legend and the father of the nation deserve this service. The money and resources for affecting this service belongs to the people and must be used to guarantee them basic human needs that fulfil their hopes and dreams.

South Africa is far bigger and richer than Ireland. If Ireland can do it, South Africa can do it even better. If Nigeria fails to do it for its people with the billions of barrels of crude oil money they sell daily, South Africa will do it better with its meagre resources as the giant of Africa. South Africans deserve better than any nation in the African continent. The children of Soweto deserve better. The Zulus and Xhosa people deserve better. And the time is now!

If the government decide to ignore this important advice and fail its own people through corruption and poor service delivery, such a government will be putting the lives of all its' people in grave danger, especially the lives of the white minority. It will further inflame hatred and racial bias among the various races, a situation that cannot and must never be allowed to prevail.

Once people start to lose confidence in the government and its leaders, these people cannot be forced to respect their leaders and judge them positively. Respect is earned by what people do in the lives of other people. Confidence is something gained by trust and respect for good conduct and lack of betrayal or blackmail. Just like the corrupt government of Nigeria, any government that cannot guarantee its citizens basic human needs with all its resources, is a failed government.

People in South Africa have gone through enough storms and stress in their lives with hope of living through the nightmares and embracing a true democratic order that guarantees equal rights and justice. South Africans will weep no-more.

South Africans deserve equal rights and justice through this vibrant and qualitative social welfare services to guarantee them their fundamental human rights to basic human needs. Only this kind of gesture on the part of government is a true expression of the spirit of 'Ubuntu'. The government must set the pace and show good example for others to follow.

What the people needs now is a better life for all, and without regards to colour or race. How far the government efforts has been to meet the hopes and dreams of the people in this country is something for which only time will tell.

Though South Africa is unlike most other African nations, it should endeavour to be a normal society not taken over by crime and violence. The numbers of police or security operatives will not in any way stop crime and violence, but will only increase tensions in society as crime and violence escalates astronomically.

What will fight crime and violence is a good quality social welfare system reforms that guarantees good life, joy and happiness for everyone in the society. 'Security' they say, gives room for conspiracy.

This is something the leadership in South Africa must take into serious considerations because the business of leading this country is a very serious business that requires very serious sacrifices and serious solutions in other to mend the seriously broken fences in the lives of its entire people.

Special attention must be paid to the lives of the black people who today are the only ones seen taking part in violent protests amid the high rate of crime and violence in the society. All these negativities are not good for the image of this great nation.

The problems being created by the black people for the government through protest marches and demonstrations, is an indication of the problems that were created for them in the past which need redress and must be addressed to meet their hopes and dreams.

It is not time to apportion blame to anymore, or go on goose chase for something that is not there after about 20 years of freedom and democracy, but a time to act now, and helps guarantee with immediate effect, social security and equality of life.

South Africans need fundamental human rights to qualitative basic standards of living, basic human needs, and all those aspects of life which will lead everyone to the part of peace, truth and justice for all. There is need for human dignity, so that they can be empowered with this human dignity to make choices in the fulfilment of their hopes and dreams in life.

Joe Odiboh

Chapter 4
A Cocoon in the Sunset

The fact that it is only the black people the world watches with dismay on the television screens protesting over poor service delivery, poor wages, and poor conditions of life in South Africa is a warning signal that there is need to address the issues of social equality. As Nelson Mandela once said, "Freedom and democracy is meaningless without freedom from hunger and poverty". True freedom and democracy embodies freedom to dignity of human lives to basic human needs.

We all witnessed how the black soldiers of the SANDF strike as workers took an ugly dangerous turn sometime ago in South Africa, and we also see people who often hold the system hostage, demanding for better wages and living conditions. These are all enough for the government to know that the country is not united, and all is not well in the business of inequality in the country.

One way of guaranteeing equality of life like I have always said is mainly through a qualitative social welfare system for all in this country. This is the greatest task of government in service delivery, which will help drastically to remove the imbalance and injustice that exist today.

This will help to reduce drastically the culture of crime and violence in that country. While the social welfare system provides for the people basic human needs, the government must create programs and policies for compulsory education and skills development tied as attachments to preconditions in the social welfare system.

This is what they do in Ireland to ensure everyone is empowered to become employable. This kind of policies ensures that no-matter how young or old you are, no one is idle. You are either working or going to school while the government will do their best in assisting the people in job placement and job creation.

This is how a real government of the people with true democratic order functions and provides for everyone without bias or regards to race or social status. This is what is called social equality for all. Using the word social equality is far different from practicing it. This is what is lacking in South Africa and in African leadership.

Another way of adding value to life is through universal free education for all, manpower training and skills development with the institution of cooperative societies in the various aspects of national growth and development. It is very important to make primary education compulsory for all the children with free feeding schemes to ensure that no child attends school in hunger or starvation.

Free feeding schemes is kinds of incentive that will help children remain focused in school exactly the way it is in the South African hospitals where every patient on admission is adequately and properly fed with balanced diet in hospitals. This is another way of producing a generation of enlightened and educated children, pupils, students and youths with civic responsibilities to the nation. South Africa is not doing badly in this regards.

These children should be allowed to travel to other countries in Africa and around the world on student exchange programs that will open their minds and hearts to the understanding of the life in other nations and learn the ways and cultures of other countries to become more acquainted to the reality of life on earth, and enable them to have the knowledge and vision to become better persons and citizens on earth.

We are aware of the incidents of child violence in our schools and disrespectful attitude of some children to their parents and in the society. We know how some children are already into drugs, sex and rape, and how some children go to school with knives and guns to hurt other children and kill each other and their teachers.

By sending them to other countries through student exchange programs, it will afford them the opportunity of learning the ways of other nations, how to grow up responsibly and respectfully, and expose them to the reality that people are not violent, disrespectful and that school is not a place for crimes and drugs where children kill each other or shoot and kill their teachers.

These children will come back home after the programs, humble and fulfilled with better sense of belonging and nationhood, prepared to share their experiences in the nation to other people with the spirit of patriotism.

All these will erase from their minds the racist tendency and background under which they were born and raised in this country. It will further help to create unity among these children in society whereby breeding a new generation of children united together with a common purpose and a deep sense of nationhood.

By doing this, the future is made secure for our children in this country and the hopes and aspirations for the future is further energized, whereby solving half of the nation's future problems in this regards. This is the first step to unity in diversity for our country. We must understand that "Unity is Strength", which should be the motto in government programs and agendas in allowing the people to see the cocoon in the sunset of their lives.

Universal free education is a right of every South African as the key that will lock the doors of ignorance and poverty in their lives and empower the people to have a secure future for national growth and development. Though we know that all my propositions are difficult tasks, they are feasible tasks that can be embarked upon by responsible government.

This is what the task of government must be. The task of government is not about the repetition of old ways and old systems and government agendas from one decade to the other without moving forward. Programs and agendas must be creative and innovative to meet with the current growing needs of the 21st century.

The reason why the people and society in most parts of Africa are tired of African leadership is lack of innovation, lack of creativity and lack of government programs and agendas that addresses the current needs of the people and do not in any way provide for basic human needs. Nigeria and most countries in Africa are sleeping governments, irresponsible leadership and nations without organized systems of government.

What our leaderships also do and repeat from time to time once they assume office is to repeat idle promises continuously in the same circle of emptiness and conventions of building a few roads, repair some health facilities, reconstruct some bridges, build a few schools and health centres, and try to maintain existing infrastructures. The issue of social welfare that deals with every individual life is never given due attention.

They do all these with corrupt practices of kick fronts and kick backs to enrich their pockets. They use this opportunity for inflated government contracts. It is all a circle of backwardness and complete waste of time.

They compliment all these by maintaining the existing civil service, collect taxes, and repeat a decayed system of backwardness and torpidity in our national lives, with the culture of fraudulent and corrupt practices because they have not taken upon themselves the responsibility of providing for the education of our children, and basic human needs that fulfil the promise of African independence.

They are there in government not knowing what to do with government funds and resources, not working hard to raise more incomes and develop our human resources to meet with our hopes and dreams.

A country such as Nigeria producing millions or billions of barrels of oil daily is supposed to become more responsible and responsive to how useful our natural and human resources are to the state, how valuable the income from crude oil sales is to the government if it was a responsible government truly working hard to meet basic human needs for the people in Nigeria.

I keep using Nigeria as an example of political failure in Africa because it is my country of origin, a place where I was born and grew up in to become a secondary school art teacher, a country that have failed my generation, the past and future generations.

The saddest thing about the Nigeria system and structure is that the past, present and future generations of Nigeria have imbibed the spirit and culture of their fathers, their attitude and beliefs and remain as people not ready for changes in their lives.

They think that changes mean how much money and wealthy individuals have accumulated, and how this money is acquired is no one's business. Success in this country is how big a house or a car is, how expensive their clothes and shoes are, and how much money people carry around in suitcases or Ghana-must-go bags.

Nigerians are very enlightened people, intelligent and hardworking with great hopes and aspirations in life. The question is how we use this intelligence, hard work and wisdom of life, how we reason and our attitude to life. The flight of millions of Nigerians from Nigeria is caused by our quest and human greed to search in other nations the remedy to our failures in life and in the life our nation.

These failures in our lives and in the life in Nigeria are certain things that can never change in Nigeria unless human attitude changes and we define our priorities and set them right in the face of corruption and human greed. How we reconcile these differences is a matter of what we truly wish for our nation Nigeria and for all our people.

Unfortunately, most people in Nigeria are very ignorant and oblivious of what is development because no government in Nigeria have ever exposed Nigerians to real development programs and agendas because of corruption and irresponsibility. Those few leaders in Nigeria seemingly being seen as the progressives are simply leaders doing very little things, very simple things and are playing on the intelligence and mentality of their people. These masses in the society are being fooled to believing that the government is doing something because their predecessors did absolutely nothing.

Progress is measured not on the merit of the activities of past and present leaders, not by how much programs and agendas are created by government for better conditions of life but by addressing basic human needs.

Nigerians back home do not know that real urban planning and development is missing in their lives, lack of energy and electricity or regular power supply, lack of roads, lack of good traffic system, lack of mechanized agriculture or food supply, lack of agro allied industries, lack of manufacturing industries, lack of proper education and educational facilities, lack of medical facilities or medi-care, lack of emergency facilities and emergency procedures, lack of effective communication facilities, lack of goods and services, lack of effective tax codes and system, lack of anything good in Nigeria.

What they see as development are pockets of makeshift cosmetics and signs of wonders. Only those Nigerians in diasporas or those living outside Nigeria in the civilized world truly understand the issues I have raised, and understand what is development. In their ignorance those who have remained all their lives in Nigeria will not only argue and reason blindly on these issues when raised, the only question they will ask and can ask is "What is the way forward?"

"How much do you have?" "What did you bring home from overseas?" "What is he saying?" "The guys don colo". They will say all kinds of unimaginable things and nonsense so bad that you will never wish to go back home and become part of such people.

Even if you tell them and show them the way forward, they will still continue to ask for the way forward, because many of them have eyes, they cannot see beyond what money they can get as individuals in the way forward to boost their ego.

If you show them the way, they cannot see or hear you properly because they have never known a way forward, and the government have never moved them forward in truth and light to a better tomorrow. The only way forward they have known all their lives is the corruption and greed of succession of governments in Nigeria.

This is why we cannot isolate and divorce South African problems completely from world problems and issues. South Africa is not the only country with problems on earth, and it is definitely not the country with the highest rate of crime and violence even in Africa, and in the rest parts of the world.

The only problem why we bemoan crime and violence in South Africa is because it is a country that have gone through much problems created by the apartheid regime and do not in any way deserve further crime and violence after freedom and democracy. This country is too good, so beautiful, and too nice to be allowed to go down in history by incidence of crime and violence.

South Africans deserve better than that, and it is sure to conquer all its adversities. This is not why we cannot wholly blame government efforts as not being in the right track, but the problem about life in general; is that life in truth has never been fair, nor has true justice ever prevailed in the life of man anywhere in the world.

We seem to pretend or bemuse ourselves about issues of freedom and democracy, knowing that freedom and democracy has never truly been used as solutions to man's problems and in the resolution of our worse nightmares.

This can be seen on how the government operates in different nations, with different problems and gross violations of human rights, or the state of the entire world today.

There is hardly any nation without a problem or crises these days. The problems we face in one part of the world are not too different from those in other parts of the world.

They are either similar in one way or the other or they reflect same ideals, same needs, same wants, with religion, tribalism, politics, economy, and all other factors playing one role or the other to define our national problems and crises.

Whichever way or what our national problems and crises are on earth, there are certain things that are similar, certain ideals that are required for national growth and development, and certain basic human needs that everyone on earth require in other to make life more meaningful on earth and make the world a peaceful and better place to live.

In our search to make the world free and democratic, we must enforce the spirit and virtues of freedom and democracy which cannot be divorced from education and fundamental human rights with access to basic human needs for everyone on earth.

South Africa is only my potpourri for writing this story or book in expressing my thoughts on problems and issues regarding the way life go right here on earth, because charity begins at home.

Though I am originally from Nigeria, the love I have for South Africa is so much and so great that I regard and adopt South Africa as part of my home and upbringing. It is a country that gave me hope when I felt hopeless in life. It is a country that energized me and reshaped the course of my destiny. And for all these, I owe a great service to the people of South Africa.

There can never be freedom or democracy, human rights and justice if there is no universal free education and basic standard of living which guarantees a qualitative basic human wants and needs for everyone in every nation.

Freedom and justice starts with freedom to a good and fulfilling life where everyone is the same before the law, and before man and God. It means freedom to good health, good house, good education, good food and balanced diet, good clothing, and freedom to self determination to fulfil our hopes and dreams in life. That is the true meaning of freedom and democracy.

For the benefit of politics, our politicians or leaders were supposed to use our freedom and democracy to represent us and provide for us all these needs with our natural and human resources on earth.

In this context, I can rightly say that most of them have stripped us bare of our freedom and democracy and limited it to the use of words and terminology, that freedom and democracy is simply government of the people, for the people and by the people.

Many of them campaign with this biggest lie in human history. This terrible lie is the genesis of all human problems and tribulations on earth. If we go to the Holy Bible in the Old Testament, there is no much difference in the problems or crises in the Holy Bible, crises of wars, civil strife, rebellions and genocide which we experience today on earth.

Iraq which is Babylon is still burning. Syria which is Assyria is being torn apart by hailstorms from heaven, or President Assad's jet bombers and ISIL. The Middle East and the Arab world are in deep crises and revolt.

Anti Christ rose and have left his followers and others to continue his terrorist network all over the world as suicide bombers. Indian and Pakistan are neck to neck over ownership of Cashmere. North and South Korea are in nuclear contest of fear and favour.

Japan and China is sword drawn over little plots of islands in the Pacific. Egypt is again terrified by a political plague and military dictatorship. Libya is in deep trouble. Iran, Lebanon and the allied forces are not ready to let my people live in peace because of the Israeli and Palestine crises. Africa is in turmoil. Australia is on fire.

America and Europe is faced with natural disasters and economic conflicts. Earthquakes, earth tremors, hurricanes, and volcanic eruptions are doing much damage to the safety and security of lives and properties in most nations. Many other nations have become places of mourning, sorrow and tears.

The reason for all these is that humanity have not changed from their sinful ways or evolved to become better people on earth with good leaderships. How then can we preach the gospel of freedom and democracy on earth when all these things reflect the face of the earth today in the way life goes on right here on the planet?

Birds are free to fly in the sky, yet there are limitations between up and down, as these birds need to come down and perch in other to feed. They always fly back to those places where they know they can find food, and to those people who are always there to feed them. God have provided for man from the time of creation, like the birds and animals and creatures of the earth everything we need to live comfortably right here on earth.

God did not limit the air we breathe to anyone or to any creature or living things. God ensured that the air was free to all living things because of its importance to life, including water and land.

Today, we fight over all these things God gave to us free of charge and limit the resources to life in our human wants and needs only to a few sets of people on earth in the name of freedom and democracy, or dictatorship and totalitarianism.

This is the revelation to all our human problems we face today right here on earth. This limitation to life and human existence is caused by leadership problems in the universe.

In this revelation, we cannot truthfully define freedom and democracy as government of the people, for the people, and by the people, because the people are the ones who are suffering on earth, they are the once being abused, and deprived of fundamental human rights and justice.

The people are the ones being raped, robbed and killed. The people are the ones that cannot receive proper health facilities, starving to death, working their ass day and night for the government, and remain the victims of all the problems, destructions and death which life have put in our mouths to chew and eat with very bitter tastes.

We fight for land and the waters of the firmament, and we think we own the water and land God created which me met on earth and which we must leave on earth when we die. We fight each other for everything good on earth, things we could have shared equally to provide for everyone, enough land which can accommodate the peoples of the earth.

As if all these things are not enough for us, we have began to explore space, hoping to inhabit other planets, and using the resources of the earth which are enough to provide for all our human wants and needs for space programs and missions. Then we waste the rest of the earth's resources on military soft-wares and hard-wares, arms, ammunitions, and weapons of human destruction.

This makes humanity like birds of the air vulnerable to man and its leadership, who can decide at will to catch and kill them, harm them, cage them, or release them back to the freedom of the sky or life. This is exactly how it is in the life of man in our freedom and democracy.

Even as birds, these creatures still know the danger in life, hence they still believe that since men have learnt to shoot without missing, so have birds also learnt to fly most times without perching.

Man enjoys the privilege of controlling the life and affairs of man. This is what they use leadership and government for, and not in the provision of basic human needs for the human race, and ensure social justice for all.

Freedom or democracy is a very good thing, very reliable on principles yet, it is like the merciless or merciful whips of fate as the case maybe, or may not be, depending on the leadership. It is nothing short of being used as instruments of man's indignation to man in controlling the affairs of man, in whichever way it likes in the limitation of the will of God to all mankind.

If it was possible to catch the air and limit it to only a certain people on earth, man and our leaders would have since starved us of the air we breathe freely and deprive humanity of this basic need to human existence. Because they cannot do this, they have created biological and chemical weapons, bombs and atomic bombs to exterminate the human race.

We are all witness to all these scientific and horrific ambitions of man and some of our leaders to create these weapons of human or mass destruction, instead of creating those things and aspects of science that can ensure the satisfaction of basic human wants and needs in our lives.

How can the government of a nation that cannot feed, clothe or house its people, or cater for their health needs and education, empowerment or guarantee them better life, spend billions of US dollars, human and natural resources of the state in planning and implementation of a program for decades that will harm and destroy mankind? Yet, such a government says it is representing the interest of the people. This is the kind of leadership we are talking about in world affairs.

Today most Americans are fighting to ensure that submachine guns and ammunitions are not limited or banned in the United States without fighting to ensure that hunger and starvation is not the problems in the life of their people.

They are not fighting to ensure that the technical problems associated with Obama care is eradicated and ensure that the program is a success. They are not fighting to eradicate the incidence of crime in society by banning individual ownership of certain guns.

This is a society that the world emulates as the greatest country on earth. These people are not fighting to eradicate the incidence of crime and violence on earth, and ensure better life for all. Their problem is that they need guns, and for what?

Kill people? Kill people for what reasons? Are we here on earth to kill people or to help one another to have a better life?

Instead of Americans wasting the tax payer's money on unnecessary debates, it is better for them as the greatest nation on earth to show us good examples and debate about fundamental human rights to basic standard of living and basic human needs for every American and everyone on earth, and champion this cause.

By championing this cause, they will be doing this world a great service. While it is necessary to protect the weak, it is equally as well necessary to make the weak stronger by empowering them to have a good standard of living. The money spent on wars can be used to bring about peace on earth and ensure that the world become a better place to live.

Helping to fight for the poor in wars is one thing, but championing the cause of a better life for all in protecting the weak nations is another issue. I believe the weak and meek will be glad that their basic human needs are met in ensuring for them a better tomorrow. Weak and meek nations and people all over the universe need basic human needs in life and not basic human wars of protection. The cause of wars is inequality of life in all nations of the earth.

No country on earth which has guaranteed its citizens basic human needs will attack other nations with basic human needs, because there will be no reason or purpose for such attacks or wars. The cause of wars is because there is no basic human needs for all human being, and this is what creates inequality, unhappiness, injustice, jealousy, crises, rebellion, genocide, and man's indignation to man.

This is the root of all cruelty in human lives. It is the root of African witchcraft. Hunger, poverty and anger in the hearts of men are responsible for the evils of man. It is the cause of crime and violence in society.

Humanity cannot eat and drink crude oil or natural gas, arms and ammunitions, biological and chemical weapons. Man do not need to live in space or in mars, nor do we need most inventions on earth to give man basic human needs such as proper housing, good Medicare, clothing and three square meals of balanced diets daily. These are basic needs which are necessary more than even education and any other thing on earth.

This is very simple and easy, and is something leadership and governments all over the world must focus on and deliver to all their people. Basic human needs are more important than any electrical and scientific invention in creation, because people and animals including all living things have been in existence before the age of science. These basic human needs are more important than infrastructures or any program or policies of any government in any country anywhere in the face of the earth.

Basic human needs are a primary problem, and the implementation and effectiveness of this program of action is the responsibility of all world leaders. It should be the most important reason why we founded the United Nation Organization. It must be the primary reason why our leadership gather together year in and year out in their council.

It should be the reason why all other United Nations bodies and NGO's world wide should be in existence to compliment all government efforts to ensure that every child born into the world is assured basic standard of living and fundamental human rights to proper housing, Medicare, clothing, and good food with hygienic drinking water.

We do not need all these junk food and chemical water in juices and cool drinks as basic human needs. All these wastes and juices and fruits must be classified as luxuries which people can have to add value to their lives. These are secondary food items, flavours, and addictives which is optional in human wants and needs, same as all other things and human wants to satisfy their hopes and dreams.

By the UN making basic human needs compulsory for everyone in every nation, no one will be tempted to destroy anyone's house in wars or arson, because they are basic human needs which everyone has on earth. People will learn to have dignity of life and respect each other, knowing that whoever we are, wherever we are, whatever religion or race we are or belong to; we all have one thing in common; same hopes and needs, same basic human rights, equal rights and justice to basic human needs in life.

By doing this, the world will be a better place to live in, and the problems of the earth will be effectively eliminated and radically changed for the common good of all mankind. This is something that is very important as the only revelation of truth in the way forward for the human race.

Nobody on earth can solve the problems of the world because we are not perfect people. But one thing we owe humanity is fundamental human rights to a healthy life, and basic human needs. Though this task is very easy for human being and our world leaders to implement, we can at least try to implement it and face the difficulties involved in its implementation.

In those days in Africa, people use to help each other in the community as a task to build their houses, a system where the communities gather together to help any adult build a house once that person has attained the age of an adult.

Communities through communal efforts use to help foreigners and visitors to the land build houses to live in. There was nothing like homelessness or bonds and rates to do these things. Communities used to ensure that no one goes hungry or go to bed with hunger in the community.

People use to help each other in the community to ensure basic human needs. Communities use to ensure that everyone or visitors to their land has a house and a piece of land to farm on. Today people and nations fight over a piece of land and kill one another in very costly wars.

The world is made of communities all over the universe, and the world must not allow capitalist greed to kill our community spirits and deprive us of the humanity in us. This kind of feeling is something the government must harness for the people and help make it a reality in government programs and agendas.

The government can give the community the money and equipments and facilities to help build community properties, community farms, and help create cooperative enterprise. This can be properly done in community spirit in providing for each other, instead of awarding inflated government contracts to contractors for all building projects. There are people with expertise in society, and people must be trained to develop the relevant skills and knowledge necessary for community growth and development.

Farming projects can be done by each community in their lands through mechanized agriculture and cooperative farming to provide for the community. As long as every community development project is done by the community labour, the nations' funds and resources will be within the various communities all over the universe and will empower them to do their best for their various communities.

By empowering each community on earth, it makes the world busy and productive global communities. Busy and empowered communities do not have time for wars or acts of terrorism, because they are busy contributing to the social, political, and economic growth of their communities. This is what community spirit can do to better the human race. Incidence of crime and violence will in this way be effectively eradicated all over the globe. This is a lesson we must all learn from the exit of Nelson Mandela. The human face of leadership roles and services is a necessity to mankind.

This is a simple example of what governments, world leaders, and community leaders and everyone can do to change the face of humanity and make a great difference to better mankind. It is something humanity can use as weapon against the problems of the earth though most leaders especially in Africa, Asia, and South America often use democracy as authoritarians in their bid to live and die in power. Instead of living and die in power, our world leaders must live and die in progress, and die knowing that they have done their best to better mankind.

Some freedom and democracy is like the wind or storm, which takes its toll on human lives and properties with no one having real power to stop the storms or the winds. Such is the storm and stress in life we face in our world of freedom and democracy. It is often difficult to weather the storms and stress in our quest to a better tomorrow, knowing that no condition is a permanent feature in life.

We cannot continue as humanity to live in the past and remain in a permanent condition for thousands and thousands of years. We cannot continue to live and die in vain like our past leaders without making this difference now in our days on earth. The world is watching and waiting to see you as a leader set the pace in making this meaningful difference in human lives.

Using the resources of the state to make this difference is not like using your personal funds for charity. Using the resources of the earth for the basic human needs for the peoples of the earth is not something that is difficult or impossible. If one leader on earth practices this 'Odiboh Care' program of action as suggested by me, I believe you too can do it. "Yes You Can!"

Freedom and democracy goes on earth with capitalism rather than with socialism. Be it socialist or capitalist government, it is all one and the same thing like it is in the book "Animal Farm", where all animals are equal, but some are more equal than others. We know how the pigs used and abused the horses. That is how it is in world leadership.

We must not see the world as an Animal Farm where our leaders can come and go and do whatever they like or wish in human lives. We must have a manifesto and a general equal program of action for the good of all mankind. This is what the legacy of Nelson Mandela is all about.

Like President Barrack Obama of the United States rightly said in his funeral oration for Nelson Mandela in South Africa, "I have learnt from Nelson Mandela. He makes me want to be a better person and a better leader". This is the kind of spirit the world leaders must cultivate for the good of society.

Socialism and capitalism are nothing by philosophic use of words and we all know that no sociology, psychology, or philosophy book or thoughts and theories have ever found problems to human problems and needs. Even those books and philosophies that have defined basic human needs have not in any way touched the hearts of people and government to provide basic human needs. They are simply like theories for academic use in economics and commerce. The practice of this theory must become a moral code in society.

Today, I respect and honour late former President Nelson Madiba Mandela, and my special appreciation goes to the Republic of Ireland for providing for all its people and immigrants to their land these basic human needs. Other world leaders must borrow a leaf from the Irish people. We must try and make the world simpler and not sophisticated. Sophistication brings more sorrow, pains and tears in our eyes. It creates divisions and barriers in humankind. It breaks down the community spirits in our hearts and minds.

Sophistication of life makes very simple things for the people and for the community seems like climbing the tallest mountains for our world leaders in other nations of the world. Today, Ireland is a quiet, responsible, simple, and reasonable country with very quiet and reasonable people who are there trying to live in peace, and harmony with only pockets of very few isolated incidents of crime and violence. It is a country built upon the foundations of community spirit.

This is why it is very hard to see cops carrying guns even if you live in Ireland for twenty years. The kind of peaceful life in the Republic of Ireland is unique and commendable. Belfast or Northern Ireland is still forcefully under the British rule, and I believe with time Belfast or Northern Ireland will become a role model for peace and stability because of their Irish decent and relationship.

We are not animals in animal farm, but humans. We must not allow ourselves to become products of animal instincts and egos. We must do something meaningful in life for humanity. We must not allow hate and greed to dampen this vision to adopt the policy of basic human needs.

Whichever way we want to rule our people, if a government cannot carry out this simple task of providing basic human needs for its people, and get the community working, such a government must never take place. It should resign and give those who are ready to do this the opportunity to do so. This is the hopes and dreams I have for humanity.

This is the hopes and dreams humanity must seek in their lives and in their government and they must be ready to achieve and defend it as their freedom and democracy in life. If need be that as communities we must die to defend our people's rights and privileges for basic human needs in life, and community empowerment to develop, let it be a cause for which we must be prepared to die. We do not need to die to achieve this aim, because power belongs to the people. No leader is greater than his people. No man is an Island.

In a capitalist world, life is like the wild jungle where only the strong survives in the name of equal rights and justice. Whereas we all know that there is nothing like equal rights and justice. It does not exist in the practical sense of the word because it has never prevailed in any one's life. It is simply about being free and fair. But who is really free? Who is really fair? We all know the old stories of life and human existence on earth since the time of its creation.

We cannot and must never speak of equal rights and justice if everyone does not have equal rights and justice to basic human needs provided for all by their government. That provision of these basic human needs is what fulfils the promise of independence, equal rights and justice

How can we have equal rights and justice when all fingers are not equal? Knowing that this is the case; we have to make meaningful efforts to balance the equations in human lives in such a way as to make all fingers useful and functional to better the lots of all mankind. I have enumerated in very clear terms how to do this and make all fingers useful and equal because of its sizes and shapes.

The fingers are in the perfect form the way God created them to fit into living beings. In the same way, God created us in different colours, shades, shapes and sizes. We were created perfect in the sight of God. But how we respect and accept each other as one global family and community on earth and provide for all our human needs is the bone of contention.

The size and shapes of our hands do not matter, but what work the hands do in life to better our lives, and make great difference in human lives; is what makes such hands great hands. The hands that kills, steals, murders, idle, or are used for negative influences in society are evil hands, perverse hands, immoral hands, and unskilful hands.

As the choice is ours in what we do with our hands, our hearts and minds; so shall it be with what we have done with the leadership and responsibilities placed on our shoulders by our people and our God.

This is the decision we have to make as a people, white or black, or as individuals. We must regard our acts and deeds as a burden we must all have to bear on our shoulders and on our conscience in deciding our case between white and black in what good or evils we have committed our lives to in South Africa and on earth.

In deciding the fate of South Africa, we must use our hearts, our minds and our hands very skilfully in doing well for all our people in other to have a perfect and functioning balanced national growth and development, where safety and security of lives and properties are securely guaranteed.

We must always remind ourselves that though all fingers are not equal, and all colours are not the same for all the flowers of the earth, we must use our hands very positive knowing that all fingers are useful no-matter how long or how short a finger may seem, because God created our hands the way they are for the good of man.

The equality or inequality of our fingers is what makes the hand very perfect, effective, and useful in human lives to do the things we do on earth. This is why all races and colours are very important in human lives and in South Africa; a perfect example of the beauty and manpower available for human growth and development of the hopes and dreams of this great nation.

It is unavoidable that evil have inhabited the hearts of some people and some of our leaders, many of whom are enemies of the people. However, in this search by most of our world leaders to control the affairs of man, we all know that human abuse and injustice is the order of the day in human life, and the politics of man is built upon the foundations of lies and deceit, quest for power, the kind of powers that corrupts absolutely. This is why most leaders like to behave as if they were thin gods to be worshipped.

Unknown to these leaders who behave like gods, those the gods wish to kill or condemn are first given these powers of wealth and leadership, fame, and then absolute powers that go with human greed. How we use these powers becomes a moral issue.

It is what defines the institution of leadership from one leader to the other and from one ruler to the next. One thing that does not change is that no condition is permanent. The nature of life and death and the principles of come and go have taken care of that which cannot change. The real change we need is basic human needs that make life more safe and secure right here on earth.

We have seen enough powers right here on earth and man is no-longer frightened of human powers as it was in the days of Adolph Hitler. These kind of power whether in democratic or authoritarian rule is blunt, blind, and deaf for some to shape life and do certain things to ensure selfish interest. They wish to manipulate human lives in a programmed conventionality to suit certain purposes and fulfil only a cross section of certain hopes and aspirations. These are the powers of fears and failures.

Man, have never provided good leadership on earth because they have never really taken into account the need for basic human needs for all mankind. Human leadership is a human problem which drags man down to the mud unless man starts to see the face and handwriting of God in the walls of leadership.

Leadership has always been about injustice, selfishness and human wickedness and greed. Most past and present world leadership have for too long failed humanity, and this is why one problem in one part of the continent spills over to affect other parts of the world. When one finger touches oil, it soils the rest of the fingers with it. That is the way life is here on earth, same way it led to the Arab spring, or Arab awakening.

Those nations on earth who have witnessed wars, rebellions and genocide know that war is not of any good in human life. It is an act of wickedness or in self defense where and when necessary. Even so, the cause of most wars on earth is simply wickedness of the heart and soul, human greed to possess the earth and its resources, and power tussle.

Even in the war on terror, great leaders such as former President George Bush Jr. and other world leaders with their democracy have proved in their wars in Iraq and Afghanistan that war is never solutions to everlasting peace, or solutions to acts of terrorism. The wars in Iraq have proved that when two elephants fight, it is the grass that suffers.

We are all fully aware that the chemical and biological weapons which Saddam Hussein was accused to have as excuse to engage in "Operation Desert Storm" was never found to this day, and nobody cares for this injustice and for all those innocent souls who lost their lives in this unholy war. These are endless wars with endless problems and worsening situation as one terrorist group after the other continue in the wars of destruction and deaths in these war torn nations.

Syria had these biological and chemical weapons of mass destruction, and was never attacked or destroyed. Though Syria have handed over their biological weapons to the international community for destruction, the destruction done in Syria by their leader is far worse than what chemical and biological weapons can do. ISIL has invaded Iraq and Syria, threatening to establish Islamic states in most parts of the world. The United States is forced to lunch military air strikes on these forces of evil both in Syria and Iraq, at the same time trying to help fight against the Taliban in Afghanistan. When will all these wars and terrorism come to an end? When will the madness end?

The war in Syria is a war of shame and national disgrace because there was no reason for such destruction of human lives and properties. The rebels and Syrian forces alike must be blamed for this war. The rebels are not better than those they are fighting in government because they are all and the same people with same evil intents in human lives. It is no use supporting the rebels against the President Assad forces in Syria because in a country of the blind, a one eyed man is the king of the castle. If President Assad is defeated in Syria and ousted unceremoniously, Syria will become worse than Iraq, and Islamist fundamentalist may take advantage of the situation to establish an Islamic state where hate, injustice, and lack of fundamental human rights will reign supreme. What Syria needs is a peaceful resolution to their crises, mediation, negotiation, peace, truth, and reconciliation.

The destruction already done in this country over the years is enormous. We must not forget that it is very easy to destroy anything but very difficult to rebuild all that are already destroyed in Syria. It will take time and enormous resources to rebuild Syria. This is why this insanity must come to an end immediately unless the Syrian people have no true love for their country. The war in Syria is a useless and wasted exercise, an accident that should never been allowed to happen in the first place.

It is time for all warring factions in Syria to sit down in shame and bemoan their nation. They should shake hands and hand over their weapons for storage. It is time for a compulsory ceasefire on both sides because both parties and all those involved in this war have no interest of the Syrians at heart. It is a war of pride and self ego.

It is time to come to a negotiated settlement in the Syrian crises because there are no victors in this fight but only losers. The Syrian people are the victims and losers in this war of shame and national disgrace. It is time for these human serpents to down their weapons and put the interest of the nation above their self ego or opinions of leadership. It is time to start to think about the reconstruction process and reconciliation. There is no other way forward for the Syrian people than to come together and work together to build a better tomorrow for the Syrian people.

It is no use supporting one group against the other simply because President Assad must go. Even if Assad is gone, it does not change the mind set of people or change the reality of things that Syria has disintegrated and destroyed. It does not build the institutions and properties and infrastructures already destroyed. It does not bring back the dead.

Syrians must wake up from their nightmares and embrace peace, truth and reconciliation. The country must retrace its step and come to the realization that the reconstruction process is a great task ahead of all Syrians. It is very easy to destroy but difficult to rebuild. The Syrian people have blinded themselves from the reality that this civil war is doing no one any good. The stone that they saw coming has blinded their eyes. Yet I know that a stone that is seen coming does not blind one's eyes. It is time for the Syrian people to rise up and say no more wars, and begin the reconstruction process. The world has used the Syrian crises as political game play because they do not really care for the Syrian people. That is why the war was allowed to continue for so long. It is a mockery of the Syrian people because nobody cares whether the Syrian people lived or die. When the Syrian people do not care what happens in their land and destroy their own country, others such as the ISIL, and other terrorist groups and war mongers will come and join the Syrian people to help destroy their nation. This makes it important for the Syrian people to have a change of heart and become reasonable enough not to play the fool with their fatherland and begin the reconstruction process. Nobody will do it for the Syrian people except Syrians.

This reconstruction process is a harder task than the destruction process. President Assad is just one single individual in Syria but the warring factions must think about the millions of Syrians who are victims of injustice in this unholy crises.

The Syrian rebels must understand that Syria was not Libya, and that President Assad was not Col. Gaddafi. These are two separate people in separate nations with separate destinies, and separate hopes and dreams. The foolishness in certain aspects of life is that most human beings often tend to act and react as sheep in certain situation and circumstances. Certain people are like flocks of sheep being directed and misdirected by the herdsman towards the slaughter house. In a flock of sheep, when one sheep jumps into the road towards an oncoming truck, every other sheep jumps along with it. This is the situation as witnessed in the so-called Arab spring.

When we look at the outcome of this Arab spring, those who benefited from it are the press and media who fanned the burning flame of revolution and counter-revolutions. Egypt military came to their senses. Tunisia came to their senses. Libya is finding it hard to see how foolish they acted except that Col. Gadaffi was a dictator and an evil man. Gadaffi fell so easy and flat because he was a very greedy man, and those the gods want to kill are first made mad, deaf and dumb to the plights and yearning of their people. Gadaffi thought he was a god, untouchable, indestructible.

Egyptians are crying for the return of their split milk that can never be. Bahrain is lucky to have escaped from its own self destruction. At the end, the situation and conditions of life in these Arab nations which went for the Arab spring are far worse than it was for them during their days in the so-called bondage. Many of these nations may never find peace in their lives unless they come together as a people to redefine their future and destiny. They must learn from the mistakes of the past to become better masters and effective captains of their ships.

Saddam Hussein was a dictator and a war monger, a very dangerous man. He was not Osama Bin Laden. He fell because he thought he was the god of Iraq. He went from grace to grass because of his arrogance and pride as a thin god. Col. Gaddafi did not learn any lesson from the fall of Saddam Hussein. He was a close friend and allied of Nelson Mandela, but he never learnt anything from this great legend. His pride and human greed drowned him in a pit of hell.

They were both typical cases of world leaders the gods wished to kill. The gods made them greedy, mad, deaf and dumb. They had lost every sense of humanity in them and they had lost their sense of vanity. The gods in their land wanted them dead and made them deaf and dumb to the plights of their people. They had thought they were gods, and that they were larger than life. The same thing happened to Hitler of Germany, Gen. Sani Abacha of Nigeria, Mobutu of the DRC, Samuel Doe of Liberia, and several other leaders.

They were so blinded by power and refused to leave the stage when the ovation was loudest. When destruction begets destruction in the wars of power tussle, we can rightly say that the poor innocent grasses are the poor innocent souls who get caught as victims of circumstance in these wars and terror.

Many people see terrorism as an act of ignorance and emptiness, sadness, and madness. It is a way of human revolt against the institutions of man, against injustice and inequality of life in society. It is a way of advocating worse demonic evil as a possible replacement for a world order that is in it-self a system of evil breed and dubious intents.

Terrorism is an advocacy of doom or apocalypse. It is not an Islamic or religious agenda. It is a fundamental anger and hate that brews in the hearts of men against those aspects of life that have never been truly fair to humanity. It is a war by humans against humanity. It is a war for the extermination of the human race in hope that we can be recreated, re-born and reincarnate into a brand new world in the Garden of Eden.

Even for those aspects of life that are good and fair like going to school to acquire knowledge and education, gender equality, the work of UNICEF in providing vaccines and health needs for children, babies and pregnant mothers; it is sad that sadists who are enemies of humanity will act out of ignorance to kill and destroy anything good in humanity, because they have lost faith in life. It is madness to see terrorists targeting schools, churches, health workers, or any aspect of life that gives joy and hope to the common man.

This is why terrorism is not a good concept or an alternative to anything good. It is very difficult to understand why evil must beget evil. It is unreasonable, perverse, and unskilful acts. Most of these children being educated or given health needs by UNICEF are children and babies belonging to the terrorists. When these terrorists are sick, they run to the hospital to get medical attention.

They don't lay back at home with their guns and bombs and die in pains. They get help and medical attention in other to stay alive. This is why some people think these people are having mental problems when they kill school kids and burn down schools and heritage sites which houses their own Islamic manuscripts on Prophet Mohamed. How can you set fire to the history of your religion? This is madness.

This is the more reason why these terrorists are not representing any religious body or group. Their activities are un-Islamic, perverse, immoral, and unskilful. Islam preaches universal love and protects its books and historical artefacts and monuments.

People who have lost all hopes and dreams in life are the ones who become terrorists, because they are tormenting from within their hearts and souls, possessed by demons, burning with desires of the Satan, because the body of death is full of the creatures of death. Anything that can make a man or a woman to take his or her own life, and take other innocent people along with them, is something that requires scientific and psychological research and analysis, and not wars to resolve.

Hunting for terrorists to kill is like hunting for someone who is looking for death and praying to die. These are people with death wish. How can you kill people who have volunteered to die? These are people who want to die, who love to die, and who wish to die. By killing them, you fulfil their hopes and dreams because they are bodies of death full of the creatures of death. They don't want to live in this world anymore because they are tired of the kind of life we live here on earth.

Even so, it is true that it is not every terrorist that wish to die, many of them are afraid of death, and these people in the terrorist group use innocent souls, especially polluting the minds of children and women, indoctrinate them and force young men and women to their untimely death to satisfy their acts of terrorist agendas. Whichever way or impression I have of these terrorists, one thing is very clear in my mind, the show of love.

So, what we need to do; is to capture them and beg them to live. Teach them the value of life, and help them to live good life, a better life for all. Let us teach them the beauty of human life, all the good things of life, and why it is good to help save other lives, and not kill people. Love, conquers all things where wars have failed. This lesson of life and goodwill can begin in detention camps which houses a lot of terrorists.

I believe this is where the show of love, goodwill, and the need to help one another comes into play in the life of all mankind in our fight against terrorism. *Once they understand the powers of love and life, they will refuse to kill themselves; instead they will embrace and appreciate their lives, love their lives and love others.*

Since we know that Islamic faith preaches universal love, and that experience have shown that people in the Islamic faith practice the power of giving and charity more than the Christians, we must not forget that Moslems are not only more charitable, but more dedicated to each other's needs.

They are more prayerful, united and dedicated than Christians worldwide. This is because it is a religion that is united as one, unlike the Christians with all kinds of denominations and multiplicity of prophets, intercessors, apostles, pastors, and God knows what?

Islam is in better position to set the pace in ensuring basic human needs for all their people and worshippers. They cannot do this by conflicts in their countries, but by a determined resolve to uphold the spirit of giving and sharing. We need to help the world to stamp out the incidence of terrorism by a few dissident groups in that religion.

They must understand that terrorists are giving that religion a stigma to tarnish the good image of their religious faith and belief. They must unite together as a front and say "No to Terrorism". With the help of Moslems worldwide, I believe terrorism have no place in humanity.

We must understand that acts of wickedness or terrorism is not a religious issue but a human issue of certain wicked souls trying to deceive others and gain cheap popularity and follower-ship by using religion as a means to achieve their evil and ignorant intentions.

Any man that indoctrinates a youth, a child, and teaches him or her how to die as a suicide bomber, does not love that youth or child. Anyone who teaches and preaches hatred and death to humanity is an enemy of life.

Such people should set themselves on fire if they are tired of life and die quietly, alone, and see if death is a thing of beauty and joy. They should not kill innocent souls because by killing innocent souls, they act as cowards. Mohamed was not a coward. Those who wish to die should die alone if they are no cowards. If the bombs they carry are so nice, they must blow themselves up alone in the wilderness so that they can go straight to Allah.

Any terrorist that targets people and innocent souls is the greatest coward on the face of the earth, because he or she is afraid to die alone. If they are no cowards, they must bomb and blast themselves alone as heroes to make a point on earth regarding their unhappiness.

We must remember that everyone wishes to go to heaven or paradise, but nobody wants to die. In a case where people wants to die in the name of terrorism or religious faith and belief, it is better to show them the heaven or paradise right here on earth so that they can embrace life fully and use it for a good cause, and not for terrorist acts and activities.

If we teach those willing to die and take innocents souls along with them, the need to live, and teach them the value of human life, and make them to live this kind of good life with basic human needs, and have basic human rights and justice for all right here on earth; perhaps they will not be willing to die and kill us.

It is very difficult to see someone with a very good and fulfilled life wishing to die. Instead, they run from death or anything that threatens their lives, because they love life, and do not wish to lose it and all that they have and their families.

By refusing to die, they will not be planning or plotting against anyone anymore. In that case, the incidence of terror will be effectively reduced to its barest minimum or eliminated for the good of society. Love, without good intentions in a fulfilled life is a dismal love, a dead frustrating hellish love.

Democracy and love are two things that were suppose to go hand in hand. If there is love, the leaders of the world must do unto their citizens exactly as they as leaders live their lives with their families.

One thing is to be a leader, and another thing is to be a ruler. Anybody can be a ruler, whether illiterate or a moron and imbecile. It takes no wisdom to be a ruler and rulers are usually the ones who rule their countries or nations with total abandon and disdain; dragging down their nations daily into the pits of hell.

Being a leader takes a great deal of wisdom, understanding and true love for their people. Such leaders must be able to deliver the goodies that fulfill the yearnings, hopes and aspirations of the people. It requires a great deal of equality and justice to exhibit the show of love to people who have placed great trust and hopes on their leader.

Only leaders filled with so much love in their hearts for their people, love undiluted, love un-mortgaged, the kind of love that adds meaning and values to life; that leadership can be said to be meaningful and realistic.

Such ideal leadership as displayed in the exemplary characters of former President Nelson Mandela, and Mother Theresa are enough to lead the way and show the light to the world the kind of love that can exist in show of human kindness.

It is good and nourishing to love and be loved, and this kind of leadership can do a great deal to better mankind. Love and leadership is patient, suffering and silence, poor and humble, innocent and honest.

Some people were born with leadership, some achieve it, and others have it thrust upon them. How the various parties express leadership is a matter of following their hearts and moral conscience. It all depends on how much they are able to fight the temptations of the human flesh and needs, the insatiable desires of corruption and greed, the powers that corrupts absolutely.

It is very easy to reason rationally and wisely as a wise man when there is no money, power and authority. At that time people tend to reason like Saint Joseph, or Apostle Paul. As soon as they are placed in power and positions of Authority, they come out in their true shades of colours.

They start like President Barrack Obama of the United States, move forward like President Goodluck Jonathan of Nigeria, and end up like President Robert Mugabe of Zimbabwe. Needless to speak about others, we all know their stories as tales of woes.

Love is a universal power, the greatest human force which is as strong and realistic like the living fires of the Holy Ghost. Love is a Holy Ghost fire which is not something that can be feigned by anyone or a leader. In love, there is no pretending, because the light and darkness can never meet.

A true leader is easily identifiable because by their colours we shall know them. One thing that cannot be understood is that man knows that no man is immortal, and life is not forever. Why our world leaders cannot find love in their hearts to do good for all humanity in the short time and opportunity they have in life, is something we find difficult to understand.

I believe they can do it, because it is very simple and very easy, something that is moral, skilful, rewarding, honourable, and pleasurable. There is no greater joy in life than to love our people, put a smile on every face, and help restore their hopes and dreams.

I know and believe that our leaders are people that can love and be loved. We all know that they do not have evil hearts and that they can change and become better leaders. We know that they can be misled by their advisers, and many of them did not know what they were doing.

We are glad today, that since they have read this book, and will read this book, or access the information here, this book will enable them to understand why they were chosen as leaders for their people. We know that no leader is proud to die with a national curse upon his or her head, and upon the heads of their family.

The chance and change is now to make amends, right now! This is not the time to continue to wallow in ignorance, emptiness, and uselessness as a leader. It is time to turn the table and do right by your people. The time has come when you must look inside of you upside-down and form that love, that true decent love that is pure and real, and use it effectively and competently to bring light and hope to the lives of your people, because you can do.

You can do well over evil, show love over hate, show humility over arrogance, show sincerity and selflessness over corruption and greed, and by all these; you are a victor who have conquered sorrow, tears and blood in the lives of your people.

Be a great warrior and champion by the fierceness of love that burns in your heart for your people. The powers of love will give you all the powers that you seek in life because it is the powers of light over darkness. It is the power that conquers everything and every creature or living things. Only love can save the planet, and save our local habitats.

Love and leadership involves the principles of "You eat, I eat." It is that intrinsic reciprocal display of affiliations between people in the show of love.

If a leader is doing great and living a good life while in power, it is equally good to share this great and good life also with the people, so that they the people too can have a good life as normal people and be happy in the society like their leaders.

In this way, we can say it is a government of the people, by the people, and for the people. A kind of democracy where everyone is a benefactor with good quality of life is true democracy. It is a kind of democracy where the leaders and those who placed them in positions of authority have a fair share of the nation's wealth and resources without complaint, and living together in joy and happiness.

But, if as a leader you eat alone while the people are hungry and suffering, and you expect peace, joy and fulfilment; such a leadership that is deaf, dumb and blind to the plight of its people, is like a carton full of worms.

It is a failed government that has let the people down. It is a government of themselves, for themselves, and by themselves, and not for the people, of the people and by the people. If you eat alone as a leader, you will die a lonely painful death on that day of reckoning without a name in history.

One of such saddest example of the democracy in the UN, is that not too long ago, NATO were quick to react and enforce a no-fly zone in Libya, and help destroy President Col. Gaddafi, because they regarded him as a terrorist, and many world leaders did not like his face and arrogance. Yet, we know there are worse leaders than Gaddafi on earth who are highly honoured today in society, far worse than terrorists.

One of such example is the case of President Assad of Syria. The world refused to act in Syria, same way they did with Gaddafi in Libya. China and Russia were being blamed for stopping UN action in Syria. Even so, we know that there are many countries and people who condemn China and Russia, but down deep in their hearts, they are very happy to see the crises in Syria escalate to abominable proportion.

They are enjoying the scenes of war in Syria, waiting patiently to take over the contracts for the reconstruction of all that were destroyed in the conflict. War or rebellion is big business to countries and multinational corporations.

This is where billions and trillions of dollars are securely guaranteed in good business of reconstruction process. The more Syria is destroyed, the better for good business and construction firms who are like vultures waiting for the carcass in Syria. In this crISIL, there are vested interests with hidden agendas, and with everyone knowing that the days of President Assad is over in Syria.

Here, we have the sycophants, the benefactors, and all those patiently in wait for the reconstruction process to begin. This is why some countries are in full support of the Free Syrian Army and sponsoring them with arms and ammunitions so that since President Assad has fallen from grace to grass, the new role players will give them the contracts and business of the reconstruction process.

They benefited in Iraq and Libya crude oil business and reconstruction process. This is the politics of selfishness and benefits in most human transactions in world conflicts, reconciliation and mediations. It is the same interest they have in Sudan.

This is why China and Russia blocked any UN resolution for military action and intervention in the Syrian crises, because they too have much to gain and understood this politics of human transactions. This kind of injustice in life is a common phenomenon in human relations where the truth is kept in silence. There are two things about justice and injustice.

One is the ability to know the truth and silence it, the other is the wisdom to live with injustice and accept it as a way of life. China and Russia understood these principles of injustice and unfairness in the UN, and in the world, because both nations are curators of injustice.

I believe both countries are more honest in the UN, because they are tired of pretending to live in a world order that is in fact built on the foundation of hypocrisy.

Both China and Russia do not like the word "freedom or democracy" because they practice the opposite in their society and decided to act against the UN using their veto power, knowing that nothing was fair or just in this wicked world. They are the kind of nations who believe that if people wish to fight and kill themselves, so shall it be.

This is why the world is enjoying the pleasures of being entertained by the Syrian crises in the Aljazeera News, CNN, BBC, and all other media and cable news network; and we know that all our news media on earth are in love with destruction and death as a means of business and livelihood. The Syrian crises and wars were like live Hollywood movie magic. It creates live news coverage daily. Who is to blame? Syrians must blame themselves because they were not forced by anyone or any nation to fight themselves.

The Syrian crises are of immense benefit to the media all over the world. It is a readymade source of news feed. The more it lasts, the better for the press. In this case, the foolishness of war is of benefit to others who are wise enough to fuel the flame of war and keep Babylon or Assyria burning.

This is why there is no good news anymore on earth in our news bulletins. Bad news is a commodity that sells faster, hotter and better than good news. Nobody is even interested in good news anymore, because there is not much good anymore in the face of the earth through poor and bad leaderships.

As the press ignores good news and good people and chase after bad news and bad things in people's lives to sell for profits to the media, people turn bad, society turn bad, leadership turn bad, religion turn bad, and everything in life instinctively turn bad for the bad of society.

Afghanistan and Pakistan have turned bad in other to stay in the news. Good people such as Princess Diana and many other celebrities were sourced for the bad aspects in their lives and chased to death by the cameras of paparazzi.

A religious group such as Moslem brotherhood in Egypt have become a political body like many others in search of leadership to be in the news, whereby destroying the institutions of freedom and democracy. The resultant effect was the overthrow of that democracy by military dictatorship doing worse evils to their people by the use of force. And from military dictatorship, the leadership moved to military democracy.

Israel is threatening fire and brimstone in the name of self defence and brutalized the Gaza people of Palestine, while Iran and its allied are threatening to bring the world to an end with their nuclear ambitions. This kind of injustice and inequality in how the world behaves is what creates suicide bombers and terrorists.

This is the injustice and inequality in the world that makes the world unjust, divided and unfair. So, the role of the media in the way life is here on earth is something that need media debate and redress in how best the media can help make the world a better place to live. This is because, the damage they are doing to humanity in fanning the ambers of all our current problems and conflicts on earth, is something that calls for total reforms.

The UN was quick to enforce a no-fly zone in Libya, but could not do the same thing in Syria to save human lives. All these and the problems of the earth is what create acts of terrorism which we as humans have created for our children knowingly or in ignorance.

This kind of injustice and unfairness in the UN and all over the world are the powers of limitations in freedom and democracy that is biased, ambiguous, and built on lies and deceit.

Knowingly or unknowingly, we allow innocent children, babies, and mothers to die through decisions we make as world leaders, without regards to the innocent souls caught in the cross fires that claim their lives. This makes us as leaders either by commission or by omission, guilty or not guilty, murderers of children and babies, and murderers of women.

What have we done as leaders with justice in the lives of all the innocent souls who are victims of all human exploitations and wars which we created in our human wants and needs?

It is so sad to see people clapping and cheering at murderers, warlords and war- mongers, simply because they are world leaders. As clappers, we the people act as hypocrites who clap in fear for those we see to be above us. We are clapping in fear of death.

We clap for them because we want them to see us clapping, and the more we clap and cheer them up, the more they grow wings and take the world for a ride, me and you. So, who is fooling whom? It is like clapping for someone who does not know or care whether you exist, or whether you lived or died.

One bad thing about human nature is that everyone knows the truth, what is right or wrong; but we are all keeping quiet because of the powers of interest groups, what some have to gain or lose in any process or dialogue.

This kind of selfish interest is what shapes our mentalities in taking action to do things that are either morally just or unjust, and ignore things we know are very wrong in human lives, remain silent and let injustice prevail.

We all know that man has good plans with paper work, and evil intentions in dealings. Most people use and abuse the good plans in punishment of others. As men, we have never been truly just or righteousness in our thoughts, words, and in our deeds. We all know in our hearts that true justice have never been free and fair in the lives of most people on earth.

It has always been a smokescreen to satisfy our human desires, wants and needs, and what people wish in the lives of other people. It has always played the role of power tussle, oppression and repression, as well as victimization. It is used as a means of satisfaction of personal ego or revenge.

Democracy, authoritarianism, freedom, and justice are nothing but terms and conditions, which have never been a product of fair play or gratification; hence the world is in great turmoil today, full of civil disturbance and death.

This is because the path we have chosen in life to follow is that of evil, far from the path of righteousness. The path we have chosen is what defines the crises we are all having all over the world. It is what defines the character of society and what we are as a people. The problems or nature of a society or a nation, defines the character of the people in that society or nation.

Africa is what it is today because of what they are as a people. If a child is very loving and good, the society will say "He is our son". But if a child is wicked and bad in society, the society will say "He is the son this ...and ...that".

They will identify the bad son as the son of John or the daughter of James. No one wish to accept being related to the bad son. The society will disown that son. That is exactly how it is with government and leadership. It is the choice of a leader to be a good son or a bad daughter, or the other way round.

Even so, we are not in position to judge anyone, but to encourage everyone by show of love both as leaders and as a people. A society without love cannot provide good and wise leaders in society. A leader without love in his or her heart cannot love the society, and cannot be loved, and there is no way of reciprocating love between a bad society and its bad leadership.

Only a good leader with great wisdom and love can show the people love, teach the people how to love, and lead the people to the part of togetherness and love. It takes a great leader like Nelson Mandela to change bad to good. Only a wise and good leader can. You too can do it, if you wish to do it. "Yes, You Can!".

In a situation where man is the judge of man which is necessary in human relations, law and order, and man is the leader and ruler of man in making decisions and creating white paper laws and rules as resolutions and agreements for the rule of law and service delivery; it is agreeable therefore that whatever agreements are made in crises resolutions, accepted and agreed to by both parties, someone out there must play the fool and accept defeat in other to reach an agreement, or for the rule of law to take place. There is always a victim in every human transaction in life.

These laws, rules, regulations, resolutions and agreements often turn around to further hunt us and compound the problems of man, because the Wisdom of Solomon was not applied in good faith in resolving the issues and problems that confront us as a people. When, goodwill turns ill, there are no moral justifications for certain actions or agreements which breeds sorrow tears and blood.

The pain of accepting certain rules and agreements in other to find lasting peace and progress, knowing that such agreements in truth were not reached in fairness, in truth, and in justice; any reconciliation effort reached in such a negative situation or accepted under duress without much choice, is sure to remain as injustice in the hearts of men. It is sure to boomerang or bounce back.

This is the complex situation in South Africa, a situation of injustice of unfairness, which still prevails in the hearts of men despite the freedom and democracy, despite peace, truth and reconciliation efforts, which has not fully truly reconciled the ways and means of livelihood in the lives of the African people.

South Africa is a producer of gold, platinum and deals on diamonds trade which is present in the land as source of the development in that country. This is a country that has got the state of the art infrastructures, and its development is comparable with any country in the first world, except for the presence of some informal settlements which has become a common feature and an eyesore in the face of progress, and in the face of injustice. Besides living in informal settlements, their condition of life is very appalling, lamentable and regrettable.

These informal settlements and poverty in the lives of these people are the unpolished and uncut nature of diamonds in the land. It implies the rawness of gold, meaning it has to go through the furnace; meaning a lot has to be done to end the poverty and poor conditions of lives in the ghettoes and poor settlements all over South Africa.

The raw nature of the injustice that still prevails in that country can be seen everywhere, knowing that no one, no black or coloured person, no South African is supposed to live that way in informal settlements or in poverty in the midst of plenty and beauty of the land.

South Africa cannot and must not be allowed to degenerate like Somalia or some other African nations on accounts of poverty.

Joe Odiboh

Chapter 5
Going to South Africa

South Africa has a population of more than fifty million people from all parts of the world, and of all races, colour and creed, making it a rainbow nation such as the United States of America.

It is a country which hosts millions of immigrants and asylum seekers all over the universe, especially immigrants from other troubled African nations.

The government have been merciful, compassionate, and understandably active in opening the doors, gates, and borders of that country to all Africans and immigrants from all parts of the world, including, Pakistanis, Indians, Europeans, British and Irish people, Asians and Chinese, and to all in the human race, with equal opportunities, equal rights and justice. This was made possible by the Madiba legacy and the spirit of Ubuntu.

By doing this, South Africa have inherited the problems of other nations in addition to their already existing problems, and have further compounded the problems without taking into account the essence of making meaningful efforts to correct the imbalance of the past, reparations, and by creating viable programs and agendas that eliminates racial bias, ethnic strife, tribalism, and bring about true integration process.

Here, further divisions are created as immigrants and people align themselves either with one race or colour and

continue in the unholy marginalization and suppression of the black people.

An Indian man, Moroccan, Egyptian, Algerian, Pakistani, and a Chinese man feel superior to the black people from indigenous African traditional system because of their colour or hair in their heads. These immigrants tend to live among their race or colour group communities with regards to colour or race.

The small businesses in this country, is controlled by the Chinese, Indians and these foreigners, while the white people are in total control of the economy and big businesses, the land, and all the major properties.

While some black people and indigenes of this society have made great progress, the vast majority of the people are just there at the lowest ebb in society, making this rainbow nation one of the most diversified in the African continent.

Even in this diversity, there is a great difference and divisions among the African community, each group in search of its own tribe, its own ways, and its own identity and pursuit of how to live and survive in this ambiguous system, confused, frustrated, and at war with themselves. This is the cause of xenophobia in South Africa.

Many people are so vulnerable and helpless because they do not know how to fit into an economic system that have no basic human needs to stabilize them socially and economically for personal growth and development.

This situation is made worse because the justice system in South Africa and the police have no regards for black Africans, and those from neighbouring countries. Africans are worse hit by injustice in every way and by every means in society.

As the greatest multicultural, multiracial, and multilingual country in the African continent, South Africa is a tourist destination with abundance of natural resources making it one of the best of the very best in the world today.

Tourists and visitors to this wonderland always keep coming back because South Africa is irresistible to anyone who has had the opportunity to enjoy its splendour, women and wine.

Everyone will agree with me that South Africa is a land of the fairy tales, where opportunities lay endless in self-determination, in arts, theatre, commerce, and in industry for residents, immigrants and foreign investors.

It is such a beautiful wonderful country like the seven wonders of the earth. However, all these opportunities are relative, depending on which kind of situation people find themselves in this country.

The weather condition in South Africa is brilliant for everyone of every race, yet unpredictable in the Western Cape, and dicey in some other regions. One moment, it is very warm or calm in some regions. The next moment, it is bitterly cold, windy and misty in other regions. All this depends on the weather condition prevailing at that time. It is this perfect weather condition among other wonders of 'Mother Nature' that makes tourism a major industry in this great nation.

South Africans understood this weather condition a great deal as part of their culture and upbringing. The Northern Cape and Eastern Cape, especially Durban in Kwazulu Natal, or Cape Town in the Western Cape is a very special place to be as tourist destination. The Western Cape is very exceptional in its natural beauty and landmarks, making it the Cape of Good-Hope.

It is a weather condition that gives hope and renews the spirit of everyone and making it a place that nourishes the heart and souls of all its dwellers, a place where people wish to live and spend the rest days of their lives as homeland.

The natural beauty of this wonderful nation, the landmark, mountains, valleys, plains, rivers, lakes, ravines, farms, beaches, caves, deep sea diving, floral, the Mother City of Cape

Town; is not the only aspect that attracts visitors; but the colourful people, the food and wine.

There are other aspects of this splendour such as the wine-lands and wine routes in Western Cape, the Table Mountain, the various beaches, swimming pools and waterways, Ostrich, birds, seals, whales, kites, water sports, cycling, motor sports, horse racing, casinos, penguins, game reserves, heritage sites, Ratanga Junction and Century City, NI City, V&A Waterfront, the Coons or Malay Quire, art and culture, the perfect and unbeatable hospitality industry, information technology, effective communication system, transportation, and the business conferencing, makes South Africa the mother of all tourist attraction sites and destination.

This great wonderland is one of the most beautiful and hospitable-nation on earth. It is a perfect art of God's creativity as a land flowing with milk and honey, the promise-land with King Solomon's Mines.

It is a country that was developed with the help of the white people, Africans alike and God's artistry in Africa to bring happiness and joy, fulfilment and hope to mankind in the Garden of Eden.

This country Garden of Eden took God special effects to create during the creation of the earth. It was the "Marquette" God used to sample the practicality of how the face of the earth and nature must look like in the various continents all over the universe. In his creation efforts, God worked on South African regions in concert with East and Central Africa to reflect on the creation of South America and the Amazons.

Here, God developed the foresight in what he believed is good in human nature and development, and applied it in the creation of the world. This makes South Africa the cradle of world creativity and civilization even though this theory has not been officially documented on the pages of "The Guinness Book of Records.

Though many historians and archaeologists may dispute this fact, some recent archaeological developments and discoveries are beginning to unearth proofs of this fact that life and civilization began in South Africa. There are proofs and discoveries of such archaeological artefacts and dinosaurs including cave art which tend to lend credence to some of these facts.

However hard they may try to prove this belief, it is important to note that South Africa is the virgin land of undiscovered archaeology, cave art, the bush-men, many of whom still exist today amidst the presence of several heritage sites.

This is a country and a place where people of the "old stone age" in shapes, bone structures, attitudes and beliefs can be seen in transformation with civilization. It is very easy to find people with "old stone age features and bone structures" in the various communities, especially among the "Khuoesan" people in the bush and some coloured communities close to Namibia.

In fact, God was fully awake and did overtime by working round the clock in the creation of South Africa, especially the Western Cape, Durban, and some other provinces.

On the seventh day after the creation of the earth, I believe God rested on top of the Table Mountain and breathed a sigh of relief. He looked downwards and merged the Atlantic Ocean with the Indian Ocean at the Cape Point.

God then gave charge of his angels the wisdom necessary to help guide the white people and the Boers from Germany and Netherlands who migrated to South Africa the vision to complete his almighty work in a craft-man-ship that was overwhelmingly admirable.

It was this will of God to fulfil his word that may have led the white man to South Africa by irony of fate and enabled them to use the inhabitants of the land in the development process which we see of South Africa today.

Unfortunately, the developers did not have the interest of the inhabitants of the land at heart when they embarked on massive development efforts. This was their sin against humanity and God their creator. They created the apartheid policy, racial discrimination, segregation and dehumanized the African people.

Some South Africans of various races especially the white and coloured people and the Indians often argue that God knew from the beginning of time, from the time of creation that if the black people was allowed to take their destiny into their hands without the advent of the white man, South Africa would have become like most other African nations today, and will definitely not be able to cultivate the natural and mineral resources to develop the entire country the way the white man did. They often argue that South Africa would have been like Kenya, Nigeria and surrounding nations.

Some black people often joke at the bars and drinking parlous that God was the one who gave the white man the wisdom and knowledge, the power and vision of science and technology in developing South Africa and all its resources to make the nation great.

Others do joke that this was the blessing in disguise, which is to the credit of the coming and advent of British colonial administration to King Solomon's mines.

Whichever way these people see these things, the black and coloured people provided the manual labour, skills and expertise, and did the hard work of building this nation while the developers provided the technical expertise and used the nation's natural resources and foreign investments for their own benefits.

Chapter 6
The Mine Workers

In South Africa, things are fast changing. Ways and means of life is growing at astronomical rate because of the change from apartheid regime to freedom and democracy for all. This has impacted to a very great extent on the life of most South Africans. This is made possible because a lot of people have been empowered by government to rise from grass to grace especially among the black and coloured communities.

In the past, the white people were mostly on top of the helm of affairs in national life, and the black people which include the coloured people were less privileged in every way and by every means.

All that has since changed and the government is working relentlessly to make meaningful difference in human lives. Despite all these, the past injustice is still stark naked in terms of the inequality in society which is something that cannot be easily wished away in a short spate of time.

One way of undoing these social imbalance in society is through continuous growth and development, educational and vocational opportunities, and the ability of the ordinary South Africans to exploit all opportunities and options open to them in self development and to aspire to greater heights in life.

Taking the past into considerations, one will realize that looking at the faces of mine workers in most mines in South Africa, and seeing their protest marches and rallies, it is apparent that most of these workers are black people in a country that has black, coloured, and white communities.

The government and companies find it difficult to put black people in high positions of authority overnight because it is not possible for unskilled labour and those in the lower rung in society to suddenly as high flyers fling themselves to high positions of authority in certain industries without the relevant skills and knowledge necessary for effective productivity and management.

It takes a great deal of time for empowerment to take root in a gradual process. It is in recognition of this fact that the government is gradually empowering its black and coloured people through proper education, manpower development, training and skills development to help them rise to greater heights in life.

Despite this positive development by government, most people in society are very impatient and intolerant, wishing that unskilled labour should take precedence over skilled labour. This negative thought and impatience in society have resulted in continuous protests and rallies, pressuring the government to do otherwise.

The process of transformation is a gradual process. It is like a farmland where the current crops must be nurtured for harvesting. After the harvest, the farm is cleared and ploughed, and new crops are planted to yield new harvest. This is why education and skills development is necessary to enforce such a change in other to reap a general fruitful harvest of all the crops in the farm.

It is therefore very necessary for the government to have a vision and it must stand strong and firm, resolved to do that which is morally just for society, and for national growth and development. It is true that our people need equal rights and justice, but it is equally true that equal rights and justice must be guaranteed to all without regards to race.

As South Africans, no particular race must be set backwards or drawn back on its knees to have equal rights and justice. This is the legacy of former President Nelson Mandela. This is exactly what the government is trying to do without victimizing any particular race to effect equal rights and justice. This brings us back to the issue of effective and vibrant social welfare reforms as a bridge to social equality, national growth and development.

It will help to reduce the incidence of protest marches and rallies because each role player is guaranteed basic human rights to basic human needs in life. Basic human needs are a primary issue in human lives, and help create human dignity. If there is access by everyone to basic human needs such as good housing, food, free medical service, free education, and pocket money for miscellaneous expenses, all other needs resulting from protest marches and rallies become secondary needs which are negotiable and cannot become the burden of government.

Only an effective, competent and vibrant social welfare reforms can solve the primary problems of government and discourage these protest marches and rallies in the labour industry which does not reflect the face of a rainbow nation.

However, the frequent protests most often in society with negative impact on the government is an attestation of the nature of employment equity or inequality in some sectors of the economy, where only the black people are the labourers in the land of their birth. White or coloured people are seldom seen with mine workers during protest marches because they are not part of the lower rung in the workforce.

This is not to say that there are no white or coloured people working in those mines. The issue is that most of the white and coloured people in the mining sector of the economy are perhaps in high positions of authority, in management,

Personnel, Accounting, Sales, international offices, technical and dignified positions with very decent wages.

While the black labourers are staking and risking their lives working round the clock, toiling, digging and sweating away their lives, raking billions of dollars for the government and those who own the mines, these black workers are poorly paid and live in deplorable conditions in society. This is why they keep on protesting, and asking the government and the mine owners to increase their wages and better their living conditions.

The government and the mine owners must not also forget that the minerals that are being mined from the earth belong to the inhabitants of the land, and to all South Africans. The fact is that the land from which the minerals were being mined belongs to these poor workers and their people. There is no much difference between these minerals and crude oil, and such minerals must be used to better the living conditions of the miners and communities where these minerals were being mined.

This is why such people like the former ANC youth leader, Julius Malema who now own his own political party and member of parliament often advocate for the nationalization of South African mines, thinking that the solutions to their problems lies with nationalization. This issue of nationalization is not a bad issue if in truth there is honesty and transparency in the mining industry.

But it is very difficult if not impossible to have transparency and honesty in big business where corrupt practices cannot be ruled out. The business of mining and crude oil trade or dealings in diamonds is a very tricky and dangerous business. It is the business of corruption and greed which is the soul of that business. Nationalization of such a business can also result in the nationalization of corruption and greed in human hearts and souls. This is the only danger in nationalization of certain business.

The business of mining is a very serious business and it should be treated as a business and not as a government primary business in service delivery or charity. I know and believe that the government is very responsible to the needs of the people in very useful ways. If need be that the mining industry must be nationalized, it must be done with absolute honesty, and determination to do this for the common good and welfare of all South Africans. It must be devoid of corruption and human greed. How this is possible is a matter of national heritage.

I believe that the South African government is a very responsible government who knows what is right or good for its entire people. Whatever decision the government might decide to take now or in future regarding the mining industry must definitely be for the good of all South Africans.

It is equally a good thing for the mine owners and management to try its utmost best to empower its workers and ensure that anyone working in those mines is able to have a better life and be able to provide sufficiently for their respective families. When workers are adequately provided for in their work places, it will boost their morale and increase productivity and economic stability in those places of work. It will lead to national growth and development.

Even so, the resources of the earth in South Africa belongs to the people, and to all South Africans, and must be used to provide basic human needs for all South Africans. In this way, the purpose for which God deposited these minerals on the earth for all South Africans will be fulfilled before God and man.

The biggest problem with nationalization of mines is the problem of corruption which is always very rife when people who have no stake in this business are put in positions of authorities as trustees and board of directors. Being put in a position of authority in a place where someone have no experience, expertise, business interest or investment is counterproductive and leads to all the negative influence in such business or industry.

There is usually abuse of power and favouritism. We can see such practices in Nigerian National Petroleum Corporation (NNPC), Nigerian Electric Power Authority (NEPA), and Nigerian International Telecommunication (NITEL) which were all failed government agencies in Nigeria.

All these nationalized businesses in Nigeria, and as we can see in most African countries are corrupt, total disasters, and have failed to deliver effective and competent services to the people in many decades. This is the problem with nationalisation of businesses where people seem to turn business interest to private interests.

This is not to say that the failure of nationalization in Nigeria and most other African nations is the same with South Africa. I believe whatever is done in South Africa is done better than Nigeria which is a system without any form of moral foundation.

We cannot even begin to compare Nigeria to South Africa when it comes to issues of corruption. We cannot exempt South Africa from corrupt and fraudulent practices, but that of Nigeria and most African nations is growing at astronomical progression. It's just that our people have a very bad habit of abusing the business of government for personal gains, rather than for national interest.

This can easily be seen in the way we manage the business of government in most parts of the African continent, if not in every part of our continent. This is the danger and problem with nationalization. Even so, nationalization is not a bad thing in principle or practice, and South Africa can borrow a leaf from other civilized world, and possibly follow the Norwegian model of nationalization policies and processes.

When a business of government is made private, there is much interest and hard work to ensure the success of such a business which is accountable to the government in terms of agreements reached in the process. However, this kind of system is also not immune from corruption as there are benefactors and various interest groups whose business is to make money at the cost of their own conscience, and to the detriment of their workers.

It is this business of dog eat dog in the money making process of investments and investors that is responsible for the abuse of workers' rights and poor wages. Mine workers all over the world are mostly victims of this practice and they work so hard and risk their lives to make a hell of money for the mine owners and their government.

Despite the efforts of miners to increase productivity, the mine owners are always complaining of poor profits and always threatening to close the mines if mineworkers demand for their rights to good working conditions and raise in wages.

The mine owners have formed the habit of threatening to fire or lay off their workers or cry wolf over what millions of dollars they lose during workers strikes. They weep over the billions of Euros they lose during workers strikes and protests in a single day, more than enough to pay decent wages for their workers in a whole year.

This is where some of us become confused. It is something we cannot understand. If the mine owners can lose so much money in one single day of industrial unrest, yet they complain that they are unable to pay decent wages to their workers in one single month.

While the mine owners and the coloured and white members of staff and management, including those in government are living in decent houses, in good homes, and having very good and dignified life with their children and relations, these poor diggers and black mine workers are living in shacks and cages with their poor families and impoverished relations, suffering and smiling at their jobs, asking themselves questions in their hostels why life have to keep treating them this way both in the apartheid era and the prodemocracy period.

They ask and question themselves, but they cannot find readymade answers to their individual questions. They try to find out if it was their destiny to live the way they do in their shacks, caves and hostels; unable to find hope, unable to survive and live like decent human beings. They try to figure out why the rich must get richer and the poor must get poorer? They pray in silence and yearn for hope; but hope is hard to find.

They start to wonder when the freedom and true democracy they fought and died for will bring a better life for all and the promise of a greater tomorrow for them and their families. No matter what they thought or felt, they were nearer to no solutions to their problems as poor workers. They wish they could live like their masters, and politicians but that in itself is a pipe dream. A mission impossible!

At times, they get angry and think of downing their tools, but the fear of losing their jobs, their only means of subsistence, the only hope they have to cater for the urgent needs of their families; then they resent that thought, holding on to their jobs as a lifeline.

They work and toil underground day and night not knowing when disaster will strike, or when they will be buried alive underground. All these nightmares in their lives, the bad dreams and the poor wages, make these mineworkers feel like they were workers of iniquities without hopes and dreams.

The management, mine owners, and the government are aware of the predicament of mine workers, their powerlessness, the psychology of their fears and all their troubles, and they smile at themselves and let this injustice prevail under trade agreements and industrial unrest.

To worsen this situation, and to give power to the bald head, some of the few black people who are in positions of authority are shareholders and partners in the mine industry. They are partners in progress at the mining industry. They are content with their wages of sins against humanity.

They encourage and help the mine owners to hold the destiny of their own black people in jeopardy. They help to ensure that their black brothers must remain in perpetual agony and poverty because they think all fingers are not equal in Africa.

One good gesture some of them are prepared to make, is to help in the funerals of mineworkers killed in active service or police brutality of mine workers killed during industrial unrest. They can help mineworkers when they are dead, and not when they are alive to reap the fruits of their labour.

This kind of unholy gestures is the true nature of most Africans in our continent. Since some black people lucky enough to have breakthrough in life grew up in poverty and became opportune to be in positions of authority, money, influence and affluence; they think every black man must suffer in life the way they themselves suffered, the way they think black men were destined to suffer with their families and relations for the rest days of their lives. It is a very rare gesture to see some Africans wishing other people to have good and successful life.

They want people to respect them for their success in life and bow down for them all the days of our lives. This is the genesis of African problems and poverty, and it is only the reason why nearly all the governments in Africa have refused woefully to provide all Africans decent housing facilities, clothing, food, Medicare, and all the basic human needs required by our people to live a free and dignified life. They want to live in dignity while we live in disgust. This is the character of failed African leaderships and most Africans in general.

They think every African from Cape to Cairo is a product of natural poverty, backwardness, diseases, sickness, deaths, rebellions and genocide. They think Africans must be Africans, defined with abject poverty, and refined to be servants and slave workers to the superior forces of power and affluence.

This is why things have always remained the way it is with most Africans in South Africa, and with our mine workers, labourers, cleaners, massagers, servants, stewards, with poverty forever.

The labour unions formed by labourers to represent their interest receive enormous wages like the big guns in the mine industry, and live very comfortable lives with their families and relations. They are no longer poor enough to represent their fellow workers.

Instead of representing those workers who elected them in the union, they represent themselves and their selfish interests. They pretend as if they are working for the interest of their workers, while deep down, they are working to retain their positions and become the buffer tanks for brewing crises and resolutions in the labour industry.

Apart from receiving decent wages from the contributions made by the poor oppressed labourers to help raise the standard of living of mine workers, some of these people in the labour unions become very lazy and represent their selfish interest, some of whom receive payments and bribes from the mine owners or government to derail the progress in life of these poor workers. This is not their fault, because most of them are in worse danger than the ordinary workers they represent in their unions.

Worse still, any outspoken or determined labour union leader in the mine industry, bold enough to fight and demand equal opportunities for all, decent wages and better conditions of service for the mine workers, is either overthrown, or killed in cold blood, murdered for the crime of fighting for a better life for all the mine workers. This threat to life and threat to the lives of their families by certain powerful forces are the limitations faced by most union leaders in the mining industry.

It is very difficult to blame most union leaders for their poor performances because they too are under pressure of oppression and repression in the mine industry hence they are forced to be reserved, and become facilitators between employers and the employees. This is why most workers must also try to be understanding and sympathetic to the plights of their union leaders. These are union leaders, like the workers, whose hands are tied.

This is an industry that is dangerously run as a syndicate because of the big money involved in mine business. It is a business of an overnight flight to great wealth and riches, where many people and interest groups, investors, and syndicates all over the world, are involved in various forms, and by every way and means.

The real role players in this business are not the owners or management. These are forces in the shadows of darkness that control this trade. These are the living ghosts parading themselves all over the universe in their limos and private jets as king makers. They have the powers to sit or unseat a government, than to mention an ordinary union leader.

This is big business that operates with stock exchange organs where shares are bought or sold worldwide to keep the business alive, and also from which the government depends upon for revenue to run the business of the country. So, this makes it a dangerous do or dies business. It is a greedy business of profits where loss makes many heads roll.

These magnates and share holders can tolerate anything, but one thing they cannot tolerate is if anyone plays or toil with their business or investments. Mine workers can die on duty, but they cannot tolerate their business to die along with those buried underground. This is how dangerous and dirty this business is in the mine industry. It is more profitable to them for the South African police to execute and kill the mine workers, than for the mine workers to kill their business.

Mine workers can live and die on duty, but the minerals in the earth being mined lives on as much as there will always be mineral resources in the earth created by nature for these syndicates.

Man knows the value and worth of these minerals, such as crude oil and gas, coal, columbine, gold, diamonds, platinum but to mention a few of them. Unfortunately, while man is indispensable, man is not worth to man the value and worth of these mineral resources, and this is why mine workers all over the world are mostly being used and abused all their lives without regards to them and their families by most mine owners.

In the advent of strikes and protest marches and rallies by mine workers, the mine owners and government become nervous, shaky, restless, and ruthless; knowing that what is at stake is worth far more than the miners and their demands or rallies.

The issue is that, if what is at stake is so important to the mine owners, it would have been good or expedient to also consider the welfare of those risking their lives and burning their calories to help mine that which is so important and at stake.

The interest of mine workers must be considered far above the minerals because the mineral cannot mine itself, except with robots. It is supposed to be a triangular business venture of mine owners, mine workers, and the government or investors; each party having a fair share in other to create a balance after the government have taken its share of the portion for national growth and development.

A fair share does not imply equal share, it simply means decent wages and good working conditions of mine workers. That is all they ask, that is all they wish, that is all they need to better their lives and help their families.

Though this is in reality possible, it is reasonable to at least pay decent wages to mine workers and let them and their families and relations have a better future and a better life for all.

Is this too much to ask? Does any miner of gold, diamonds, and platinum worth billions or trillions of US Dollars deserve to live in a shack covered with tarpaulins, or in a hostel like a refugee or an asylum seeker?

When the mine workers take up courage and decide to demand for decent wages, they are treated like terrorists, threatened, fired, beaten, brutalized, and sometimes killed in cold blood.

It is unimaginable that a man who have worked, risked his life, and dug the earth all his life, suffering and silent, poor and sleepless, sick and hardworking, made millions for the mine owners, suddenly ask for a better wage for a better life for his family; instead of giving him hope and favour, he is arrested and put in jail or shot dead like an animal in the watchful eyes of everyone all over the universe.

A miner who have lived all his life in fear of being buried alive underground while on the line of duty, is suddenly shot dead by the police in cold blood, or by criminals while returning home with his poor wages in the land of his ancestors.

Such is the inhumanity of man to man in the South African mine industry, a situation that needs redress, an unfinished business of land and ownership, or control of the resources of the state.

An industry where the labourers are only black people in a country the world sees as a rainbow nation, shows that something is dangerously wrong. Something has to be done to create equal rights and equal job opportunities for all its citizens irrespective of race, colour, or creed.

This goes a long way to show that South Africa is divided along racial line in business and industry, especially in mine business, an unfinished business of government to rid society of inequality in the mine industry, and define who owns the land and the resources, and how to use these resources for the common good of all South Africans, and better the lives of all those who work in this dangerous industry.

I believe this is the right thing to do in repairing the injustice of the past, done not by violent means and practices, violent workers strikes or protests, or by fraudulent greedy intentions; but with the true spirit of goodwill, truth and reconciliation, to ensure true freedom and democracy for all South Africans where everyone single South African have a right to choose their own destiny and self determination in life for a better tomorrow.

Chapter 7
The Domestic Workers

However dangerous working in the mine industry might seem, those who know South Africa and have lived there like many of us from other parts of the world will continue to wonder about the roles of women in South Africa.

It is a well known fact that the women of South Africa were the most powerful force who fought for freedom and democracy in that country. They were the ones who fought relentlessly and stood by their men, children and daughters to ensure that we enjoy the freedom and democracy which we have today in this great nation.

It is equally true that women are making great progress in the social, economic and political growth and development in the new South Africa, especially in the area of education, enterprise, entertainment, public service, politics, arts and industry.

The children and daughters of our mothers owe all our successes and achievements today in life to the women of this nation who deserve better from the government and all the people of this nation. We must also not forget that behind every successful man or child, there is a woman.

However, domestic work is a very thriving industry in South Africa which employs the vast majority of the women of this great nation, young or old. This industry is so important that the government have created a minimum wage policy and conditions of service for domestic workers and with retirement benefits.

This is something that did not exist in the past for black people during the apartheid regime. This kind of gesture on the part of government is a very big credit to the efforts of our leaders who have recognized the importance of women in our society, and the active roles they played to free our nation from the injustice of the past.

As this injustice of the past is being repaired, it is important to note that the vast majority of domestic workers in South Africa are black women, many of whom are our mothers, grandmothers, sisters, and great-grand-mothers with commitments in life, responsibilities, and with great hopes and aspirations to cater for the needs of society.

These women are the ones worse hit by poverty and inequality in our society, many of whom are too responsible and disciplined to engage in violent protests or rallies in making their voices heard loud and clear. We owe them a duty to speak for their silent voices in society and acknowledge their basic human needs.

Though there is minimum wage policy and conditions of service in the domestic work industry, many of these women as still being used and abused by their employers who cannot pay the minimum wage or ensure better conditions of service, knowing that most of these domestic workers are hungry, poor, desperate for a job, and prepared to accept anything to put food on their table.

Most of them are uneducated and ignorant about their rights and privileges, and are glad if opportune to find any domestic work. As a result, nearly all of them live below the poverty line, in shacks, or very poor housing and they struggle day and night working without hope for a better life or a better tomorrow. The wages they earn from their employers cannot and will never guarantee anyone a better comfortable tomorrow.

The pay for a domestic worker is the poorest in any employment industry because they do not work for companies or industries but for individuals who are unpredictable and struggling too to make ends meet in their lives. Anyone who pays someone from the pocket and with very scarce resources is sure to go through a hell of time to pay such wages.

It is a big struggle to do so because the employer is human with own personal problems and needs. In such a case, there are no standard conditions of employment between employers and employees because both parties are struggling to make ends meet and cannot guarantee anything now and in the near future. This is the dilemma of both the employer and the employee in the domestic work industry. It is an industry where both parties are desperate in demand and supply.

When somebody who is struggling to survive employs someone in need of food on the table, one wonders what role or meaning a minimum wage government policy can play between the employee and the employer. Such a policy lacks merit and cannot be said to be effective because it cannot force employers on employees.

This is where mutual trust and understanding is the real agreement between employers and employees in other to create a balance and keep the business of domestic work in operation. There is a great difficulty in imposing a minimum wage policy on someone who needs a nanny or babysitter or cleaner, who him or herself is earning very low wages or struggling to survive. It is also very difficult for anyone looking for a domestic work to refuse a job on accounts of low wages.

Here, there are millions of employers with their own problems and attitudes, employing millions of poor people with their own problems and attitudes. What we see is ambiguity and confusion in such an industry which has no standard measurement or definition in the scope of employment and management, as well as enforcing any condition of service or minimum wages.

The government seem to forget that he, who wears the shoes, knows where it pinches. The government is not the employer, and it cannot dictate to a struggling South African, how much money to pay to domestic workers because it does not know what the employer can afford or cannot afford to pay its employees.

This is where our women urgently need help through government subsidies for these domestic workers and the provision of basic human needs for all these women so that they can have and be able to make a choice in their domestic work. At the moment, they have no choice but to accept anything or any work that can put food on their table.

However, for effective wage policy to take root there must be effective basic human needs for the people to prosper through an effective social service. When someone is guaranteed a basic decent minimum wage in employment, or basic human needs through a social welfare system, only then can the government use this set standard in society to guarantee other standards in minimum wage policies especially for domestic workers.

Besides the issue of poor wages for domestic workers, most of all these women are black people, except for a few coloured people. The black women provide domestic work for the coloured people and mostly for the white people. Another thing is that these women are mostly South Africans except for some immigrants from neighbouring countries who are very few in numbers, and can be counted. Let us agree that South African black women are the ones working as domestic workers, serving the coloured and white communities.

It is very difficult to see coloured domestic workers working for the black people, or serving them like servants and stewards. This is a very uncommon practice in South Africa. In the same way, it is nearly impossible to see a white domestic worker working for the coloured person in South Africa. They can work for fellow white people if possible, but definitely not for the coloured people in the coloured settlements.

Many of the white domestic workers will not even risk going to the coloured settlements because they know the danger in doing so. Definitely, they will not survive for long and are sure to get killed if they venture to go and work in the homes of coloured people in the coloured settlements. Same is applicable to most coloured people or domestic workers in black settlements.

When we consider this kind of situation, it is no use even suggesting the possibility of a white domestic worker going to work for the black person in a black settlement. That will be seen as suicide, a domestic suicide worker. It is a mission impossible for a white woman to go and be working as domestic worker in Soweto, Khayelitsha, Gugulethu, Langa, or anywhere else in predominantly black settlements. Needless to say, it is difficult to see a white woman working as domestic worker for the black people in South Africa, unless you are the President of the country, or a very high government official. Even so, it is an uncommon site to see, except the white woman is working for former President Nelson Mandela.

In this case, one can see that a white domestic worker cannot work for the black people in black settlements because of colour, race, complex, or the danger in doing so. This goes a long way to show that we are our worse enemies because we have not truly embraced peace, truth, and reconciliation as a fully integrated society. There is nothing the government can do to remedy this situation.

The only solution to this problem is to wait and see as our children grow up in a free society and rise to greater heights in life. As our children grow up from one generation to the other, the problems of racism and segregation will disappear with time and fade into the mist like an accident that never happened.

Even so, we can rightly say that the black people are mostly the domestic workers in that labour industry, and they work in humility and diligence as servants and stewards in the land of their birth in service to other people and races. This is what makes these women very honourable and great in humanity. They are the greatest women in human history who are so dynamic and have shown sterling qualities in semblance to Mother Theresa, in their service to humanity.

The question is, can this kind of goodwill by South African women happen anywhere in Europe? Will Europeans ever accept to serve us as Africans in the land of their birth? Definitely No! This is because as South Africans, we have the spirit of kindness and meekness to welcome strangers into our land and homes, and we ensure that they have the best of life in our land.

We have the spirit of humility to serve other people and help all the strangers in our land, and ensure that they receive better treatment more than that which we give to ourselves. South African women are selfless people, always there to put the interest of other people above personal needs.

This spirit of welcoming others and serving others is the spirit of togetherness and love. It is the spirit of "Ubuntu" which has made South Africa the most humane and welcoming society in the African continent, and on earth.

South Africa is the only country on earth where the citizens and original inhabitants of the land work as servants, stewards, domestic workers, and labourers to immigrants and visitors to their land, and people who have become a part and parcel of that land.

This is something we cannot see in Nigeria, a place where everyone wishes to be the Boss or Prince, and every woman wishing to be called, Mama G, Madam Maria, or Princess.

Even in Christianity, no one wishes to worship under another pastor or priest, or church leader. Everyone wishes to become the priest, pastor or apostle, and everyone is forming individual church, everyone wishing to be the senator or Member of Parliament or house of assembly, and everyone destroying the image and the future of Nigeria with pride, corruption and greed to own the world.

At the end, we are on the run from our fatherland, seeking for hope in the lands of other people. Our arrogance and individual pride have brought our nation shame and national disgrace. Our lack of humility like a child and failure to put the interest of others and our national interest first above all things has made us the Golden Eagle instead of the Lion of Judah, or the Giant of Africa.

We have become like the eagles, always in the sky flying from one country to the other, only perching to prey on easy innocent vulnerable creatures of the land and sea in our flights to the unknown.

In Edo State for example, most of the women have immigrated to all parts of the world in search of the Golden Fleece. Many have perched in the UK, Italy, and Ireland.

Many of those women in that state especially in Benin City have formed the habit of poisoning their husbands through food poisoning and become Landladies and Madams, while obituary funeral ceremonies have become the most celebrated events in their lives. The culture of single mothers has become a way of life in most of these communities, something that was alien in the days of our mothers.

Anyway, the issue of domestic workers in South Africa is very important because these women deserve better for their humility and service to other people. These honourable women deserve more from South Africans for their mercy and loving kindness.

This is the unfinished business the South African government have to deal with, especially through education and skills development of these women. Adult education and community development projects and programs can help them a lot to aspire to greater heights in life.

It is never too late for anyone to hope and dream. If the black, white, and coloured people are all educated, no one will enslave anyone, and anyone can work for anyone irrespective of colour, race or creed. Educated people do not become domestic workers unless they are immigrants who are still finding it difficult to find their feet in society.

However realistic this situation is, the government have to abolish the idea of black, white, or coloured settlements in South Africa if it wants free flow of domestic workers of any race to any location in the country. It is admirable to look forward to this change in situation in due course because educational growth and development is taking root in society, and it is helping to transform the country into a true and just rainbow nation.

The transformation of the domestic workers industry can only be done with educating the people, skills development, manpower training and empowerment not only for the black people, but affirmative action for all South Africans. The government should be at the fore front like in education in uniting the people together.

It is racial and injustice to say lets help the blacks only, the coloured only, or create a government policy to disempowered the white people. It will not help the nation but tear the country apart. That in itself is another felony or injustice. Discrimination against the white people is another form of Apartheid and discrimination, which cannot and must never be allowed to happen.

The more South Africans of every race, colour or creed are empowered in South Africa, the better life for all in this country, and ensuring that they all live together as one, doing more together to build a better South Africa.

I believe this is the Madiba dream, one nation, and one destiny. This dream must be realized and accomplished if the business of freedom and democracy must be fully realized.

Joe Odiboh

Chapter 8
Security and Conspiracy

While we speak of justice or injustice in society within the legal framework of law and order, the role of the South African police Service and the judiciary is very important in the dispensation of justice, and the maintenance of law and order. In this system, the black and coloured people are mostly the victims of injustice in society.

Despite the fact that the police service and judicial system is doing its utmost best in the dispensation of justice, certain aspects of this system is very incompetent and ineffective, and it is not as functional like the police service and judicial system in Europe and the United States, because of the social injustice system which it inherited from the apartheid system and mistakes of the yesteryears. This is very glaring in the scope of things in South Africa.

This ineffectiveness and corruption in society reared out its ugly head during the funeral ceremony of former President Nelson Mandela. At a gathering of world leaders, someone who is an incompetent signer and someone with a criminal record in South Africa were appointed by the government as signer during this ceremony to the watchful eyes of the world. The national intelligence service could not do their work properly to ensure that such an incident never took place. This is an example of the cracks and carelessness in the security system.

However, in this circle of incompetence, cracks, carelessness and injustice in society, most coloured people with tattoo in the body or without teeth in their mouth are seen by the cops as criminals, gangsters, or people smoking drugs. This stigma which follows these people leads to unnecessary arrests and convictions for crimes many of them did not commit.

The judicial system cannot be said to be very just or reformed, and it condemns a lot of people for what they know nothing about exactly the same way it was unjust to former President Nelson Mandela, and all the freedom fighters in South Africa during the days of apartheid.

The system have not changed or recovered from the apartheid dose or trauma, and it is so terrible that victims of this system do not know what to expect. It is like a terrifying nightmare or a strange monster and a destructive mechanism in the life of the people.

Getting involved in any case in this country, especially if the case is not a high profile case is like waking up from a strange dream at the edge of another man's nightmares, and waking up to realize that the nightmares was yours, real and alive to your face. The more you search for justice, the more attorney bills pile up in your face, and once they see your purse is dry, then they drown you in deep waters.

The most dangerous aspect of the South African Police Service is the issue of conspiracy and compromise in their duties and services. There are too many bad cops in the system. When certain cops become professional liars, informants to criminals, and people interested in what gains they can reap from the police service and not what good they can do in society, such a system becomes compromised.

In some cases, before any raid takes place on criminal dens, drugs haven, and places where illegal activities takes place, some of the bad cops usually inform the criminals ahead of the time when they would be raided. This enables the criminals to prepare ahead for such police raids. These bad cops receive gratifications and wages from these criminals from time to time. They know themselves in the police service. The time is now to become better cops and better people in society. The society needs you to serve with honesty and dedication of service to all our people. We want to be proud of you and not see you as the enemy of humanity.

In certain instances, when certain police raids takes place, there are those bad cops who are there to profiteer from such raids by stealing evidence either for the criminals or for themselves. Some are just there to steal whatever they can for themselves. These cops can identify themselves right now in their tribunal of conscience because by their fruits, we shall know them. These things they steal from criminals or resell back to them cannot change their lives. It will further create unquenchable greed to want more and more like drugs addiction until it destroys their lives and careers completely. This kind of life is not what Madiba and society wished from a law enforcement officer with great tasks to secure the future of our great nation. It is time to have a change of heart and turn to new leaf. It is never too late to mend fences in the kingdom of God. The nation wants to award you a great medal for your bravery. South Africa needs sincerity of purpose in your service to this great nation.

We know that some of these bad officers often come back to return the evidence to the criminals after the raids and get paid for their services. Others keep what money or valuable they can lay their hands on for themselves and sell most of unwanted valuables and drugs or illegal guns back to the criminals and drug dealers in the communities. This is usually how they recycle the incidents of crime in society, and which is a national shame and disgrace.

There are so many other bad cops who give information about police informants, investigating police officers and members of the judicial system to the criminals whereby compromising their duties and put the lives of all those crime fighting officers, innocent citizens and members of the judiciary at risk. Apart from defeating the ends of justice, this kind of attitude causes betrayal of each other in the police service and makes enemies between cops and criminal elements. By betraying each other, we are encouraging the criminal to lose hope and faith in our service. We make each other vulnerable to attack. Any cop who betrays another cop has betrayed the police service, and could possibly become the victim of circumstance and situation created for the police service by him or herself. That is how the natural laws of justice work. If you do not stop this act of betrayal, history will repeat itself in your life. You have the time right now to stop this act of betrayal of your own brothers and sisters in the SAP.

Case files are often stolen from their vaults in police stations and from prosecutors, and such cases of missing files are rampart in the judicial system, whereby defeating the ends of justice. It is most unfortunate that these incidences took place in the past. It will never happen again. Never, never again must any cop steal its' own case files or that of other cops. I know and believe the SAP is there for the interest of all South Africans, and they are determined to put a full and final full-stop to this act of shame.

In many cases, some police officers often aid criminals to escape from police custody, from awaiting trial detention cells and from the prison. Many of these bad cops are using their position as service members to commit abominable crimes in South Africa, including their involvements in cash heist, breaking and entry, and often rob innocent citizens with impunity. This must not be allowed to happen. It is time to arise and shine.

Many others are involved in collecting tithes and offerings from people dealing with contraband goods and services, including criminal elements dealing in illegal trade and stolen goods and properties. I guess our cops are wise enough to know that this is terribly wrong.

The worse situation is that when a complainant reports an incident of crime, the complainant becomes the one to be quizzed, investigated with hope of prosecuting the complainant. The cops look for every way possible to see if they can rope the complainant with a crime. Instead of going to look for the accused, most of them go to the house of the complainant to see if there is anything illegal around they can use to get the complainant into deep waters.

These kinds of situation discourage people from reporting incidents of crime to the police. The complainants are usually afraid of not becoming the victims in crimes created against them. This is why victims of rape and child abuse find it hard to act against crimes in which they were victims. In such cases, most victims become victimized and the criminal elements become the victors. This kind of situation discourages community policing.

These are the bad cops who believe that they have nothing to gain personally by apprehending criminals and assisting in boring wasted time of their prosecution. They believe in what they can gain right now from criminal activities.

The police badge and uniform is their legal bait or tool to profit them and enrich their lives after the fall of apartheid. They use and abuse their positions of authority to the fullest potentials in the South African Police Service.

There are also the bad cops who are informants to the criminal elements in society, and sponsor them with their arms and ammunitions. Some of them report that they were robbed of their arms and ammunitions. Many others help criminals and gangsters with information and logistics and help to secure certain areas to ensure that perfect crimes are committed by their criminal allied.

Some others are directly involved with criminals in armed robberies and bombing of ATM cash machines. There are those who were former freedom fighters, ex-service men and women from the army and a whole lot of criminal elements involved in one way or the other in criminal activities in this country.

This is why the entire system is compromised because there is too much bad water flowing under the bridge in the dispensation of law and order. All these various elements are locked horn in horn for survival and ascendancy. Each system and structure in the judicial system has its own conspiracies and bad eggs which endanger the lives of most members of the police and judicial system.

There are threats to life, blackmail and counter-blackmail. There are threats to the lives of loved ones. There is so much danger in the system with every member of that system afraid of the insecurity of their lives, properties, and the lives of their loved ones. Many of these underground threats are kept in secret and in the dark shadows of their uniforms, wigs and gowns.

Everyone carries in his or her head individual problems and the danger that looms in their heads, afraid to speak out because they know that no one can protect them and guarantee them their security of life. This is why they often say to themselves, "Don't make your problem my problem". This is a common phenomenon in the judicial system and in the society.

All these conspiracies and lack of clarity, is responsible for the miscarriage of justice and the high rate of crime in South Africa. Everyone knows that the police cannot protect the citizens of South Africa effectively because many of them cannot be trusted. Funny enough, they cannot even protect themselves from criminals.

When some members of the South African police service and judiciary cannot even protect themselves from criminals, how can they protect the ordinary South African? This is the dilemma in the police and judicial system in this great nation.

The truth about the security system is that it is seriously compromised as a system where many officials do not care about the outcome of any case. People are not interested in who is a criminal or who is innocent. It all bothers down to guilty or not guilty verdict at the end.

Nobody is interested in the conspiracies and complicities of underlying events, circumstances and events which are hidden in the dark shades of the unseen. Nobody really knows or cares about justice or injustice in society. Whatever situation or circumstance victims of the system find themselves is simply a way of life. In a system of carelessness, nobody cares.

Most South Africans often pray never to encounter a bad cop, or when a bad cop creates a criminal case against you, or arrested you wrongfully. The problem starts like a joke with the police. The lawyer further complicates the case with the same mindset of a guilty verdict without looking at the merits or demerits of the case. Proper investigations of cases are never done in most cases.

The prosecutor or state attorney who in many cases is an employee of the government is mainly interested in his or her wages and not whether the accused has a case to answer or not. In law, every accused is presumed innocent until found guilty by the court of law. Here, the reverse is the case in the ways and manner society and the judicial system treats an accused.

Instead of investigating the matters further and professionally in search of the truth through investigative policing, some prosecutors prefer to drink beer, and spend their time partying away their lives with their friends and on

Wednesday night. They would rather have fun on weekends, and have sex to cool off the stress of judicial rigors. As far as some prosecutors are concerned, any case file on their desk is a guilty verdict.

All a prosecutor needed to do is to make a deal with the defence attorney. They both do not need to prepare their cases or get involved in the investigation process. To them, law was just a simple boring routine with boring people. This is mostly how it is with the judicial system in the cases of ordinary people in society. Being a free and fair system is a matter of luck, depending on those handling the cases.

The problems are not with the judges and magistrates, but mainly with the attorneys and advocates, the police service and the prosecutors. In law, what the prosecutors and defence arrives at is what the judges and magistrates accept as verdicts. The judges and magistrates are simply like moderators whose hands are tied.

We cannot rightfully say that there are no good attorneys and prosecutors; they are very few in the system. It is not that they are not good, but they are not very hardworking and competent as they should be, and the vast majority of them may have compromised their duties some day and sometime in line with the way things are in South Africa.

The entire system is being compromised one way or the other; knowing that no one really cares what happens for good or for bad in this system; knowing that everyman for himself, God for us all. The system is compromised with social injustice which exists in the entire society.

This is possible because of racial divide, and most apartheid attorneys and judges or magistrates may have felt that since the black people are in power with their black politics, the business of judiciary must be treated with scorn and disdain to make the government fail in its duty to provide equal rights and justice. They do not have confidence in our leadership and feel that a corrupt political order corrupts the entire system. This lack of faith in our political leadership is responsible with the ineffectiveness in the judicial process.

They have the feelings that apart from Nelson Mandela, the black leadership in this country is incapable of ruling the white man and its systems. This is why most of these white and apartheid members of the judiciary are deliberately frustrating the judicial system and the efforts of government to bring about social equality and justice for all.

Since there have never been any credible judicial reforms after the apartheid regime, it is a system that have no appropriate checks and balances, and unregulated. It is a system where the new breed of attorneys, prosecutors, magistrates and judges are working hand in hand just to keep things going as they were, and without stepping into each other's toes or seen in confrontation with each other, and knowing that something is definitely not right in the system they inherited.

It is a system where they all argue cases and interpret the laws in the simplest forms and formats within the context of the new found freedom and democracy. It is a system where no one really cares much about the complainant or the plaintiff and accused. Law and order is simply law and order for the sake of law and order. In this simple system, only the ordinary man and woman of South Africa is the victim of this social injustice.

They just do their jobs to the best of their knowledge and ability in whatever way they like and in whichever way they deem fit, knowing all is not well in the system. When things are not right in the country, nothing can be right in the entire judicial system. It's just simply a part of the pain in the ass of society, amidst all other numerous pains and problems of inequality and injustice.

This is why most South Africans have found themselves in one of the most unjust and difficult system in human history with no reforms. That is why I can unequivocally say that some prisoners rotting away in South African jails, and many of those awaiting trial are innocent victims of crimes and violence.

Many of them were at the wrong place at the wrong time, and were victims of circumstance created for them by the unknown. A survey or investigation in South African prisons will attest to this fact. This is why the government have to start afresh to review the institution of judiciary in South Africa if freedom and democracy must have meaning to the people.

The police and judicial system in South Africa have not changed much from the apartheid system, which gave life to injustice in society and nourished it as a way of life in society. It is a system still being run by the apartheid police with apartheid training, apartheid lawyers with unjust mentality, apartheid prosecutors with apartheid sense of judgment, and apartheid judges with apartheid jails and prisons.

Their mentality is shaped with injustice and social inequality. There is no way they can change a system that have not changed their mentality. They too are also in bondage, confused, confined, dispirited, disillusioned, frustrated, disadvantaged, and disoriented, each person not quite sure what the future holds for them and their children in the new South Africa.

The few black and coloured members of this judicial system cannot be different from the system, which even till today is still marginalizing them in their place of work. They are just there to go through the system without letting the system go through them in order to make very revolutionary difference that can change the face of the judiciary.

These are people without a voice. Even if they do, their voices will not be heard and will be silenced even before it is heard. A brief visit to the High Courts and Supreme Courts of Justice will attest to this fact. The few black people there are like little minority illegal aliens in the courts of their land.

When a very important apparatus of government tier or body such as the judiciary and police have not been transformed, and it is compromised, what do we expect from such a legal system? This is not a system that is sympathetic to human rights and justice. It is a draconic system operated with wickedness of the racial heart and oppressive souls who have no interest in the knowledge of human rights and justice.

There are very good judges and cops who have sacrificed their lives in ensuring justice for all. But only a few of them will openly come out and tell you the truth about this ugly system, which is being run like a legal aid. It is a system which is working for the sake of work ethics, and not for the purpose of ensuring true justice and fairness. It is a system that requires total transformation and drastic changes in ensuring social justice for all.

It can be said that there is no much difference between the gangs on the street and most of those people who are placed with responsibility to ensure law and order, or the defence of the rule of law in ensuring equal rights and justice.

In this system, justice is about your colour, your race, your nationality or where you come from. It is about how you look, what you do for a living, and whether the system likes your face or your general appearance.

This system has two faces in two worlds flowing side by side in irony. In one part of this world, justice is a matter of luck, hard and impossible to find, and in the other world, justice is assured. Which of these two worlds you find yourself, and which of these two faces you perceive, depends on your social conditions and circumstances in our new found freedom and democracy in South Africa.

Some members of the South African police do not know how to investigate crime to the fullest as it is done in Europe and America, and there is no investment of time and resources and expertise in the search for truth.

This is something that is completely missing in the system, except in some high profile cases. The cops are ill-equipped and terribly incompetent in the collation of facts and materials for circumstantial evidence in cases. The police think and act as though law and order is a matter of crime and violence. It is about using violent means and threats as investigative process. This is made worse when dealing with illegal immigrants and asylum seekers or foreign black brothers and sisters. These people are treated not as human beings but as properties.

Even exhibits and evidence gathered in most cases are usually not properly analyzed, and contested by the defence counsels who feel too lazy to do their legal homework. Most attorneys do not care to study their legal books very hard in defence of cases as they were meant to do, and in this process; there is usually a miscarriage of justice. It is quite different from what we see in television movie crime investigations or most series on law and order.

The police and detectives are risk takers who were suppose to exhaust their time and resources in serious investigations, in collaboration with the forensics and communities, and do a lot of analyses and brainstorming to come to conclusions, even-though such conclusions may become circumstantial or inconclusive in the court of law. The prosecutors and defence counsels were supposed to do more, take more risk, and expend their time and resources in processing their cases.

This is something that is impossible and completely missing in South African Police Service and the judicial system. We all know this fact, and we all know that the police, prosecutors and defence counsels are too big and pre-occupied with their own lives to sacrifice their time and resources in the pursuit of justice for the common man in South Africa.

Facing up to this fact, we all know that no member of the judicial system will make the necessary sacrifices and take risks in pursuit of justice for an ordinary man or woman from Soweto, informal settlements, Khayelitsha, Langa, Mitchells Plain, Guguletu, Joe Slovo, Deft, for illegal immigrants, or for the homeless people and homeless kids in the streets of Cape Town or Johannesburg.

This is impossible because no attorney in South Africa, black or white will burn the night candles, have sleepless nights, and spend days or weeks studying their law books in defence or prosecution of the common man or woman in South Africa. This is a mission that is impossible in our search for truth and social justice.

This is why the police can do as they like, because they know that nobody cares. When a system is careless, every aspect of that system is completely careless. In this carelessness, there is miscarriage of justice. This is the truth and the circumstance surrounding the South African judicial system where only the lucky ones survive.

This is why the country is faced with unbearable crime rates, jail breaks, murders and assassinations of the police and members of the judicial system. This is why the incidence of crime is not declining but escalating in geometric and arithmetic progression, because everyone knows that justice is very hard to find. In a system where there is no true justice, what we see is a carton full of worms. This is why communities are at war paths with the police and judiciary because they cannot be trusted.

This is why the entire system should be looked into and reformed to meet the current hopes and needs of the new South Africa. This will help a great deal to reduce the incidence of crime and miscarriage of justice in our search for truth, peace, and reconciliation. Mandela has done his work very well in his long walk to freedom, and it is for us as South Africans to re-examine ourselves, our hearts and minds and continue on our long walk to true freedom and justice for all South Africans.

What we mostly have in South Africa are violent cops, abusive prosecutors and attorneys, frustrated magistrates and judges, and a government who do not know what to do and where to start in changing the face of the judicial system. We must not be content with how things are right now, but we must embark in serious reconstruction process. There is a lot of work to be done. No one can do it for us now, but only ourselves can free our own minds.

In the midst of all these, the government is afraid of not falling as victim to this system. The government is more careful and cautious in dealings with the judicial system than the ordinary citizen of this nation. The government do not want to be seen as tampering with the judicial system and processes. If that being the case, the government must set very good examples in its general conducts, and show us the light of hope to a better tomorrow.

Without seeing the bright light, the light of hope, I believe we will continue to wallow in utter darkness. Who do we turn to now to lead us? Let us turn to ourselves because we all have the power to bring light and hope to all humanity. We can start now in South Africa. We can extinguish the hatred in our hearts and condemn acts of segregation and injustice in society.

Because we have not done this is why the judicial system in itself is segregated in style. We have those attorneys, especially the white attorneys who have excused themselves from the practice of criminal law, because they know the danger in this practice, and that the practice of criminal law is highly compromised. These are attorneys who do not wish to get involved in the dirty business of bad cops, crime and violence. They want to practice law in peace.

Many of them have shifted into company or commercial law, property law, labour law, and those aspects of law that guarantee them safety and security. They hide under these aspects of law to promote themselves to mainly cases heard in the High Courts or Supreme Courts of Justice. In these High Court cases, they pile up bills for their victims knowing that there are properties and assets available to pay their attorney fees and bills with the loss of houses and properties.

The few available ones ready to take up criminal cases go in search of case related to hard drugs, gemstones and other illegal money making deals or cases. These are the big cases with the big money. Others focus on Accident laws and pay themselves from the blood and pains of accident victims with Road Accident Funds.

The remains go for defence of criminals with the big money in high profile commercial crimes. Based on false information provided by the police, they lie in court and create false arguments to defeat the ends of justice. Others focus on claims and insurance claims.

In fact, they all know what they are doing because they are very clever people who are taking advantage of the weakness of the judicial system and processes for their own benefits. After cases in the courts, they smile at themselves knowing that in every weakness there are benefits.

In this judicial process, nearly everyone is at ease while their victims are no-longer at ease. They are just there in court to do their work and earn their wages. They have nothing to lose. The real losers are the ordinary South Africans, the poor masses of this country. Everything becomes like a conspiracy, crookedness, a legacy of injustice and unfairness.

This is why not many attorneys will waste their time to read their law books in defence of an ordinary black or coloured person? Definitely, not many of them will do so, especially when that client is nobody in society. A 'Nobody' is someone without a voice and without human dignity. More also especially when the accused have no money and the government is the one paying for the attorney service through legal aids. So, it is loyalty to the government who is paying the bills. It is the bills that count. It is all about the money, and disloyalty to the helpless accused that is often regarded as a nonentity, and a menace to society.

Who wish to waste time to defend a poor helpless fellow? That is the kind of question that pops up in the minds of most people in the entire judicial system when dealing with cases of law and order. The judiciary feels that any black or coloured poor person who is not a politician, celebrity or high profile case deserves to rot in jail, especially foreigners or asylum seekers without a voice in society.

Most of all these conspiracies are possible because the police and judicial system itself is divided on racial line. Most black cops are made to work in black communities, coloured cops in coloured communities, and white cops in white communities, with a very little mixture in race as not to make this fact very glaring. Same with the judicial system in regards dealing with court cases.

White judges and magistrates are assigned to white dominated areas, or white communities. Same is the case with coloured judges and magistrates. Because communities are segregated, the judiciary is equally segregated. Institutions are also segregated.

If things are not done this way, some elements in the communities will target the opposite race and destroy their career or assassinate them in the line of duty. All these officials are very careful in the line of duty knowing that they are being targeted by criminal elements in the society.

All these affect their duties and distort their sense of judgment. The only place where these officials are respected or recognized in society is in their law courts while on duty. Off duty, they are like anyone-else, vulnerable to attacks and criminal elements. They do not have the protection they deserve in society. It is a common sight to see a magistrate or judge going on foot from their court after duty to take a mass transit bus or train back home after work with the common man in the street.

It is cheaper and more convenient for them to travel by bus or train than face the traffic in their cars which are usually either parked at home or in bus stations or train stations public parking spaces. It is easier for criminals to target them. All these affect their sense of duty. They are afraid to keep watching their backs because of their kind of work; hence many of them prefer to be careless in their line of duty with their work. Nobody wants to die for a case in which they have no personal benefit or interest.

This is how simple and vulnerable they are in the judicial system. This is why they are very careful too how they deal with cases because they cannot watch their backs the rest days of their lives. All these explain the possibility of compromise in cases because no one knows what happens to them or what they encounter or do after work. Nobody cares about their lives.

When a case is high profile, publicized, and the elements involved are well placed people in the country, such as businessmen, politicians, and celebrities, such cases receive priority attention, and white judges or very good black judges are mostly put in charge of such cases for the good of society.

It is generally believed that cases dealt with by white judges have more credibility and such verdicts are more likely to be accepted by society. In such cases, money speaks louder than voices, including cases in High Courts and the Supreme Court.

It is very dangerous to trust some members of the South African police and the lawyers. As soon as you make the mistake to trust them and follow their legal advice, you will find yourself in a square round box. They will laugh at you and move on with their lives as if you never once existed. This is why it is better to defend yourself in any case and speak your mind in truth, than to face the danger of asking an attorney to represent you in any case.

Most attorneys in South Africa pretend to be nice and take all your money until they reap you bare and dry; then they will castrate you and roast you alive. You will not know what happened to you in any case you present to court either as an accused or a plaintiff, because there have never been serious reforms in the judicial system.

Accepting a legal aid lawyer is like suicide, or self-defeat. Call it legal aid or legal jail; there may be no much difference after-all. The best thing a legal aid lawyer can do for you; is to ask you to plead guilty so that your sentence or punishment can be negotiated. Otherwise, if you allow them to represent you, then I am very sorry for your fate. Only God or luck can set you free.

The South African Police Service, Private Security Industry, and the Judicial System are trying hard to eliminate the incidence of violence and crime in society, and stand out as the most viable employment industry.

However viable or vibrant it might seem, security seem by the clock to give way to conspiracy and insecurity of lives and properties. It is a system, which seem to be at war with its own people. On the other hand, the people also seem to be at war with the system meant to bring about peace and sanity, law and order, human rights and justice.

It is like cat and mouse relationship, or that of monkey and banana. It is a system where there is no mutual trust and understanding between the people and the police or judicial system; each party in search of each other's neck and blood.

The South African Police is very well armed, ensuring that every cop has a gun both on duty and off-duty.

They are well trained in crime prevention and crime fighting except in investigative policing and prosecution. They are highly skilled in areas of riots, violent or peaceful demonstrations but definitely not in proper investigation of crimes.

In their efforts to combat violent crimes, and public disorder, they act like apartheid cops in any crime relating to violence and public disorder, because they themselves are very violent and are disorderly in their fight against crime and public disturbance.

Many of them are very ignorant about current affairs, and they have no knowledge about life outside their locations or communities. They are very ignorant about the world affairs and cannot tell you the geography of their neighbouring countries, or where certain places are located within South Africa.

Many of them do not seem to care to know the world outside their hemisphere or domain. They are proud to tell anyone that they were born in South Africa, and will die in South Africa. Like the people in the coloured communities, many would say they were born in District Six by the Table Mountain, though they preferred to die and be buried in their coloured communities.

Most of this ignorance was created for them by the apartheid regime, a system that had blindfolded their eyes and shaped their minds to certain beliefs and shaped their lives with certain attitudes and habit difficult to break in the discharge of their duties as law enforcement agents.

Many of them are very racist in the way and manner they conduct their duties, others are tribal, and xenophobic. Some do not know their duties and do not care about the due process of the law. Some of these cops are the black empowerment and affirmative action cops recruited after 1994.

Very many of them cannot read and write or take statements in proper English language. You have to speak, read and write their local language or Afrikaans to receive good service. This language barrier, often bring about confrontation or bring about lack of service delivery in the police service. When it comes to volunteer workers, this problem is made worse in the police stations located at the informal settlements or black and coloured communities.

In the midst of all these are very humble and good officers, law abiding, and responsible. Many of them are honest and very hardworking in performing their duties effectively without race or bias within the due process of the law. These are the good cops in the South African Police Service who are committed to their jobs and are ready to make sacrifices for effective service delivery even at the cost of their own lives. They are the ones who give hope to the future and build trust in community policing.

These are men and women who have dedicated their lives to the highest cause in ensuring that the South Africa people fought and shed their blood for, will not be overtaken by criminality and vengeance, nor will they allow it to degenerate into chaos and anarchy.

These are men and women who have sacrificed their lives and social duties to their family by ensuring that they defend the rule of law, and work day and night to ensure that there is peace, safety and security of lives and properties in South Africa.

Many of these good and dedicated cops who are in minority are often set-up by the bad cops who are somehow affiliated in dealings directly with gangsters, drug lords, and hardened criminals, and are often killed in active service.

There is a great deal of injustice and conspiracy in the South African Police Service, and in the Private Security Industry. Many cops and private security officers are often targeted and killed by criminals for their hard-work, sincerity, crime fighting and prevention; others are targeted and killed simply because they are officers of the law.

Worse still, most criminals target these cops or security officers because of their guns. A few others are killed in revenge for the injustice suffered by some convicts in the hands of the law. Good cops often get killed for fighting to ensure that justice prevails.

We all know that cops and security officers are not usually safe in their uniforms in informal settlements, and are forbidden to live and visit certain areas in South Africa. If they do or move around carelessly in certain areas, they will be shot dead by criminal elements in such areas.

This kind of situation is so obvious and precarious in society where South Africa is concerned. There have been incidence of criminals attacking and bombing police stations, target and kill police officers in police stations or their duty post, and eliminate detectives or investigating officers prosecuting their cases in court. Some shoot cops on drive-by killings, or even by the robots or traffic lights for the fun of it. Many have been compromised, targeted and killed in cold blood.

The judges, prosecutors, state attorneys, defence counsels are not spared in this regard, and are often targeted and killed. This is why everyone is very careful in the way they do their jobs, and about places they go to. It is always good to be on the alert at all times, both on duty and off duty; this is why many cases are compromised for fear of their lives or the lives of their families.

Some cops are only interested in speaking, taking, and writing statements from complainants in their local languages, because the English language angers their heart, making it ache from apartheid abuse of the past. These cops hate the white man's language so much that they take the anger out on their fellow African brothers and sisters who cannot speak their local languages.

The sad thing about some cops is that they are so racist that they allow the historical disadvantage of the past to cloud their attitude and better sense of judgment, forgetting they are cops, and worse still, there is no one or any system created to rid these cops of these negative attitude and language problems in the police service. Though there may be systems to correct these ills in the police service, it cannot control human thoughts and feelings.

The private security industry is a thousand times worse, terribly unfortunate when it comes to xenophobia or man's inhumanity to man. The training they get is meant to empower black and coloured people to get security jobs easy. If it was a one or two years course, I believe not many of them can have the patience to stay and learn for such a long period, and it would have made them more serious about their jobs than about race, colour, or issues of the historical disadvantage of the past.

Some of these officers are from the villages without proper education, and they abuse and use the security industry as an end in itself to express their anger towards apartheid and foreigners. Some of these private security officers and some cops simply do whatever they wish, and bring about more injustice in the entire safety and security system.

The system used to correct the abuses and misconducts of security officers, and the police officers is hardly effective because any complainant stands the risk of being assassinated. So, reporting an abuse, injustice or crime is as dangerous as prosecuting a crime.

This is the circle of crime and violence, so bad, so dangerous that no one is safe or free from both the private security officers, cops, and the criminals alike. It's all about crime and violence in the private security industry, or SAP where only the strong survives.

However dangerous the circle of crime and violence might seem in South Africa, the efforts of these officers is also commendable. They work round the clock 24hrs in their fight against crime. The government and the private sector have done so much in providing more than enough vehicles, arms and ammunitions, armed response units, effective communication system, and mobility, camera installations nearly everywhere, crime fighting equipments, and nearly everything required to make South African Police Service, and the private security industry the best and the most equipped and effective in African history, better than most countries in Europe and most parts of the world.

South Africa is like a police or security state because of the presence of visible security officers everywhere day or night, armed response units, cops, patrol cars, traffic cops, undercover cops, police choppers, crime prevention and monitoring units, cameras monitoring units, and a whole lot of other related bodies working day and night to make the South African security system the state of the art in crime prevention and crime fighting.

The communication system of the SAP and private security industry is a very effective system, and the good thing being that anyone arrested by a cop, must be taken to court within 24hrs to face the wrought of the law, whereby eliminating the incidence of wrongful detention. The court is the most powerful system in law enforcement and prosecution.

The court is very merciless and heartless, usually unfair in most cases, because they seem to see any South African as violent and capable of any crime. Human rights and human dignity is expensive, and hatred is uppermost in the hearts of some judges and prosecutors.

To create a balance between justice and injustice in South Africa, some apartheid laws still exist. Their apartheid attorneys, advocates and judges are still running the judicial system. Most of them have channelled their injustice to the preservation of their economics, business, properties, and investment of the white man. There is a great deal of conspiracy in the judicial system against the working class, especially those at the lowest ebb.

This can be seen in credit cards issues, credits and lending, buying things on credit, bonds and mortgages, the ways business operate, property business, and the way business work with the law courts to enforce economic slavery of the working class.

In fact, nothing has changed that much from economic apartheid because, the law and judiciary ensures that black or coloured home owners and shoppers are ripped bare by draconic laws and judicial system that have turned the ordinary South African to an economic slave.

The judicial system in South Africa is a system that is dubious with two- face. It is a system that is not defined by principles of the rule of law, justice and equality for all. It is shrouded in the dark mysteries of something dangerously unknown, un-trusted, unrefined, and unpredictable. It operates like the laws of the wild-wild west where only landowners and businesses are assured of justice.

It is such a complicated system where most of the attorneys, advocates and the judges work hand in hand with business to create a nightmare for the working class, especially, those in the lower class, and in property business and managements.

Property business and management is the most fraudulent and unjust system created to take back properties people have paid the bank mortgage for over a period of more than two decades through body corporate who manage such properties with impunity and fraudulent means and practices.

Buying a property is one law, but managing the property is another law, so dubious that they create every way and means to make residents lose these properties after paying their bonds for over a period of more than two decades. They come in styles such as renovation, and give bills so fraudulent, and impossible to pay, clouded in attorney bills and interest rates which doubles the amount of the property, and use the law courts to make the residents lose their properties to the management or so called body corporate. This has happened in Radiant Mews, Lake Road, Grassy Park, Cape Town.

They start renovating flats by simply smearing paints in the outside of the flats and create a fake electronic gate for the properties especially when they know the residents have almost finished paying their bonds to the banks after more than twenty years of payments of bonds and rates. At the end, the body corporate use the law and attorneys to make the homeowners to lose their homes. Government is silent, and is unaware of the plights of its citizens. A great injustice is done.

Worse still is how people are wrongfully arrested, wrongfully accused, and wrongfully detained, and wrongfully convicted by the law courts. While South Africans have fought for true freedom and democracy, it does not include economic freedom; it does not include judicial freedom, or freedom to own what they have worked for all their lives without storm and stress.

It does not include the freedom of the black people to take back their land or mineral and natural resources, and all that their boss has invested in. It is the freedom of the white man to posses all that they took from South Africans, the land, investments, businesses, properties, and retain all the best things of life in the new South Africa.

In this rainbow nation, the white clouds is for the white man, the yellow clouds for the coloured communities, the blue clouds for the Indians, the green clouds for the new role players and the Chinese, while the black clouds hang over the heads of the black communities.

If the black communities ask to see the white clouds, they are butchered and murdered in cold blood by the police in self defence. This was what happened not too long ago in the police massacre of more than thirty-four platinum mine workers in Rustenburg who were protesting over pay rise.

This kind of police service and judiciary that butchers and jails its mine workers with apartheid laws must be reformed and a new system created to replace the injustice in the police service and judicial system. The government need to reform the police service and the entire judicial system to meet with the current needs in society and bring about trust, the rule of law and justice to end the incidence of crime and violence in society.

Chapter 9
Unity in Diversity

The memories and experiences of 2010 Soccer World Cup in South Africa is an attestation to the beauty and glory of this great nation if only the nation can unite all its resources together as one for the common purpose of goodwill, one nation, and one destiny. The unity of all South Africans in the integration process in earnest began with the 2010 soccer world cup, and almost ended with it, because of the imbalance and injustice in society.

The 2010 Soccer World Cup was a blessing in disguise; a learning process of what unity can do to change the face of South Africa. It was a turning point in South African history to show its entire people that united as one, integrated, and putting aside the differences in race and colour to a common purpose and goal can turn a nation to a progressive state, with economic growth and development.

It was an occasion which would have afforded all South Africans the rare opportunity for once to truly reconcile their differences and take a dynamic step to put everything in South Africa on one table and share it equally in such a way as to guarantee everyone equal share, equal rights and justice. It is a missed opportunity, which South Africans ignored and turned to a cosmetic surgical operation to prove to the world that they were united, knowing it was not a long and lasting legacy of unity in diversity. The greatest injustice a nation can do to itself is self-pretence.

Coming together physically without coming together socially, economically and politically was like coming together without joining together. Joining together like one big family is like coming together as one to share the wealth of the family rationally in such a way that everyone has a fair share and a better life for all members of the family. In family union, there is love, togetherness, and the spirit of Ubuntu. This is the spirit of love, caring, sharing, and coming together as one united big family. This implies that unity is strength because anger against a fellow South African must only be felt in the flesh and not in the bone. Anger against a brother is only felt in the mind and not in the heart. This thought is the bedrock to true peace and reconciliation in that country.

When some members of a family are very poor and wretched, working day and night like servants and stewards, while other members of the same family are very rich and opulent; a house that divides against itself shall not stand the test of time. It will not be a happy family. There will be jealousy and anger in that family among family members because a hungry man is an angry man. In such a family, love will turn to hate, and hope will turn to despair.

This is a very dangerous situation because members of your family may be your worse enemies, and when they strike at you, they can never miss their target, and you will not know what happened to you. Before you even think about it, it is already too late to cry when the head if off. This is usually why in African witchcraft, your closest relations and loved ones are your worst nightmares. We in South Africa are our own nightmares through injustice in society and the various acts of crime and violence which threaten to derail peace and progress in our fatherland. It is important therefore to harness our national pride and resources for the common good of everyone and help secure the common bonds that bind us together as a people. If we allow the anger and hate in us to continue to create racial bias, this is very unhealthy for national unity, national growth and development.

Such anger and jealousy is poisonous and can lead to murder, manslaughter, assassinations, afflictions, and some family members poisoning the others in other to inherit some share of the assets of their deceased relations. Others will exterminate other family members and cause them untold misfortunes in other to end the circle of domination in their families.

This kind of hate, anger and jealousy in the family is the root of African witchcraft in indigenous African traditional society. Such anger and hate in families can be seen in countries such as Nigeria and many others spread across West Africa, East Africa, and Central Africa. It is the root cause of rebellion and genocide in Africa today where losers wish to destroy the winners, making everyone become losers at the end in the life of a nation.

African witchcraft is born out of hate, jealousy, and anger against a relation or neighbour who is either progressive or too down to earth. It is very evil and destructive and bears no good fruit, nor does it lead to togetherness and love.

This is the kind of hate and poison that is born in the hearts of most black and coloured South Africans, the white people and the Boers towards each other, and towards the government of their country. It is a situation where love is expensive and hatred is cheap in their national life.

This lack of love in society has resulted in violence and hatred, where no one is to be trusted by anyone. This lack of trust in society is another problem in society because where there is no love there is no trust among people.

South African witchcraft is predominant in the black and coloured communities, especially where people do not need to fly about at midnight or astral travel to hurt their victims. Here in this country, your enemies strike at you day or night without mercy, face to face, and in the presence of everyone. They do not use their fingernails to rip out flesh and blood from the human body. They use knives, guns, broken bottles and anything they can find as objects to cause bodily harm and death. The sight of blood in this country is like the sight of butter and bread.

Here, people do not hide their hatred and hurt people with impunity, and kill without mercy. There is also the kind of witchcraft which brews anger, hatred and racial bias towards those whom the vast majority of South Africans feel have impoverished them, and those who are enjoying the wealth of society without regards or compassion in their hearts towards the suffering masses of this great nation.

We all know that the government cannot solve this problem alone. It has no law against witchcraft or the anger and hate in human hearts. It cannot force the rich to give to the poor. It cannot force the white people to give up their belongings and share them with the poor black and coloured South Africans. This is a matter for the tribunal of conscience.

The government cannot take away the economy from the hands of the white people and share it equally among the poor. It is something that morality demands people to use their initiatives and make the meaningful sacrifices necessary to make meaningful difference in the lives of all South Africans in ensuring a better life for all. A better life for all means united we stand, together we fall. It means togetherness and love. This is the solution to national growth and development as well as true integration process.

The major solutions to South African problems requires moral codes and values that everyone has to follow in other to meet set objectives and goals for the common good of society.

What use is there in inheriting the whole world knowing that one day one will die and leave these things behind?

The answer is a moral question of human sacrifice. This is the moral question of vanity upon vanity, which people should take stock of and ask themselves every day, and every moment which road they should follow. Must we take the road of anger and hate, or the road of love and peace? We have a choice as citizens of this great nation to become good and humble masters of our destiny and great masters of our fate as a nation.

"For how long will black South Africans continue to suffer in the land of their birth while those who took away their belongings and their lives are busy smiling, enjoying everything they took away by force? How long will this injustice prevail?" This is where the government has a role to play in empowering its people through a very good and viable social welfare reforms system that caters for the needs of all, and bridge the gap between up and down, front and back, and between white and black. Only a good and viable social welfare can cater for the basic needs of all the masses of this great nation. The social welfare system is only the antidote to a healing process of human hearts and minds and stop people from thinking and remembering the injustice of the past in society.

If the white people of South Africa can also have the heart and find courage in asking themselves these moral questions of what is good for society, it will be the first step towards peace, truth and reconciliation. It is not the time to start to think of who wronged whom or what went wrong; who hurt whom?

It is time for sober reflection; for re-evaluating our minds, and asks yourself, what good you can do for South Africa to help repair the injustice of the past. It is time for sacrifice believing that for every good you do to better the cause of history, the greater rewards await you and your generations in time to come.

It is not time to apportion blame or regrets for what happened in the past. The past is over and gone. It is time to believe that everything happen for certain good of society. It is for you to search for that good inside you and take the pleasure of becoming a hero in the kind of good you do for society. You can do that now, right now!

History will remember you my dear Boers, not for how big your farm was, or how much investments or properties you accumulated on earth; but for how many investments you made in human lives like Nelson Mandela, how many properties you built and gave to the poor people in the land you called your home. You will be remembered for how many people you taught how to farm and to fend for themselves in society.

You must weep no more for mother earth my dear farmers. We have come to cross the Rubicon. The mother earth in which you farm will only bless your body and rest you in peace at the end of the road not for how many mouths you fed with your farms for personal gains or profits, but how many people you taught how to farm and empowered to farm in the land long after you were gone.

The mother earth of South Africa will bless the fruits of your seedling and all your children to become fruitful and happy in life for how many mouths you fed when they were hungry, when there was none to care. The mother earth will bless you for all the good you did on earth in your homeland.

Weep not my Beloved South Africans, shed no more tears for the evils of apartheid, weep not for Nelson Mandela, but rejoice for what good Nelson Mandela and apartheid have done for you, and endeavour to do greater things by turning around the fortunes of this land.

A thousand kilometre journey begins with one step. Take that step now into the moral foundations in building a true and just South Africa. Every positive step you take is to the greater good of all South Africans.

Develop a positive mindset and remember that you may know how you are today in South Africa, but you may not know how your children will be tomorrow in South Africa. Make the sacrifice now for your children for what tomorrow will bring.

Secure for your children a greater future not by focusing on your children, but by what you can do for your country to cater for the needs of all South Africans. This is the selfless good and part you must take to a secure future for your generations. What we are as individuals and as a people will define our future. The time is now! Act now!

Seek for the goodness in you and discard the hate in you. Embrace compassion over wickedness of the heart and soul. Let not your heart lead you to a shameful and fruitless exit in the history of your fatherland. Together we can do more to better South Africa.

For too long people just keep repeating the same life, living with the same mistakes, in a meaningless and fruitless life. Whether you are poor or rich, life is life, and many live but once. What then have you done with your life in the life of South Africa? What then was your dream in the life of this country? It is time to dream.

Is your dream to eat, sleep, enjoy and die without doing something special, something fulfilling and humane, something that will make you raise your head very high above your shoulders before man and God? Question yourself. Heal yourself. Save yourself from the injustice of the past by what justice you can bring to balance the injustice.

For every action you take today in the course of history, there will be a reaction in the course of history. Take that action now to pioneer the reparation efforts in South Africa. History will be on your side. History always favours the just.

Make hay my people while the sun shines. Enlighten yourself with the evils of apartheid, and with that knowledge; take the first step in turning the evils of apartheid to the good of apartheid. Yes, you can make that difference now and move the country ahead to a better future.

Crime and violence does not pay. The seeds you sow today in South Africa are what your generations will reap tomorrow. It is never too late to mend fences in the kingdom of God. It is never too late to sow the seeds of greatness in the new South Africa.

Bless God for giving you the rare opportunity to be alive, to be able to reason positively, and give to yourself the strength and power you need to make a great difference according to your power and your strength.

The greater the good you think in your heart, the better your mind, the greater the strength and manpower you have to come out in the open and make the sacrifice this country needs to show that in every one, there is greater good than evil.

Goodness has no colour, race or barrier. It is simply the foundation upon which the garden of togetherness and love is watered in the life of man. Choose goodness over colour or race and open your heart to the possibility of togetherness and love. What you open your heart to, is what your heart will desire for this great nation.

Open your heart to peace, truth, and reconciliation. Open your heart to what meaningful contributions you can make selflessly for the good of this great nation. That is something you will be proud of, something for which generations will cherish you name.

Many evil men and women have come and gone. They came and conquered, and they possessed the earth. Today they are all gone with all their powers and all their wealth is in vain.

They are long gone with all their evils. Do not become one of them. Do not become a part of them. The time is now to do away with all your evil deeds and make a U-turn to help renew our hopes and dreams in this great nation. The evil ones will go as the evil ones are gone.

They are gone forever with all their evils that dwell in their bones at their final resting place. What do you want to leave behind in your bones? Can you inherit the earth? If you can and wish to inherit the earth, do something great now for the inheritance of the people you leave behind, something for which posterity will glorify your name forever.

A Few white people who adopted the apartheid policy in the apartheid regime, and agents of colonization are the ones who today make people refer to the white people for what they did. Yet, we know that white people are not evil people, they are very good people like most of us. They too were victims of a system created for them by the evil ones. Most white people were not happy with the evils of apartheid, nor did they support it.

Some fought against it and made sacrifices, yet today we simply refer to all as the white people. As white people, you have the opportunity now in life to be free to do something great for your freedom and democracy in South Africa. The opportunity is now for you to disassociate yourself from the evil ones and write a new page in history for the white people of this great nation.

Arise and shine above the mist and set the pace in determining the future of your land, the kind of future you wish your children and generations yet unborn to inherit in this country. South Africa belongs to all your children; the time is now to build a new South Africa for all your children. Make the necessary sacrifice now for a new social political and economic order that fulfils the promise of true freedom and democracy for all.

Today we are all alive, tomorrow we will all be gone like those before us. Make a difference now, bold and proud that you are truly a South African. Time and tide waits for no one; the time is now to be the hero of our land. This you can do in whichever way you can, and in whatever way you know is morally just and healthy for the transformation process.

The real battle now is not the battle among ourselves, or the battle among yourselves for survival or supremacy as a race or colour, nor should it be a battle for wealth or possession to retain the wealth of society, or battle for social, economic or political domination; it should be a battle of conscience and moral values, to do all that is morally just to empower all South Africans to become better people in the face of moral decadence.

It should be a battle to rid society of injustice, crime, violence and those vices that tear the country apart, and making it ungovernable. It should be a battle to rid South Africa of the common enemy holding back peace and progress for all in the country and the common bonds, which unite us together as a people.

South Africans have no other country than South Africa, an only steak or kidney pie does not get lost in the microwave oven during lunch break. Bearing this in mind, all South Africans owe a sacred duty to South Africa, a duty of rules and regulations, or moral obligations to defend the constitution and the rule of law.

It is a duty to make sacrifices and contributions in ensuring that the freedom and democracy in South Africa is nourished and watered to grow into greater heights in life. The kind of freedom that brings hope and joy to the life of all South Africans to be proud and secure, knowing and believing life is good for all and children yet unborn.

It should be the kind of sacrifices that has root and will grow stronger year in and year out over the years to secure and guarantee South Africans their hopes and dreams. This dream cannot and will never come true if South Africans abandon their root and neglect the common bonds that bind them together as a people.

We all owe the mother earth of South Africa a duty as a people; the country which gave us life and nourished us, knowing that what seed we sow on this land will be the reward of all that we shall reap from this homeland. The time is now to sow that seed in the life of South Africa and become fruitful, yet we know that a tree that does not bear fruit is cut down and cast into fire.

No South African by wrong choice should endeavour to become a fruitless tree cut and cast into the fire. This is not our hopes and dreams; it is not the dream of any South African born of a woman. It is our portion to make a meaningful difference that counts, the type of goodwill that can give joy and hope to the common man and lighting up the flame of smiles on our faces.

The joy and happiness of any South African is the joy of a nation, the poverty in the informal settlements is the poverty and backwardness of South Africa; something we should all be ashamed of as a people. Having a good house is one thing, but having a good life or standard of living is another thing altogether.

In making our sacrifices, we must bear in mind a good standard of life for all South Africans which reflects a life well lived right here on earth. *Looking at all our gravesites; lay the souls of the faithful departed in South Africa. These were once people like us, full of life, full of hopes and great aspirations in life.*

Today, they are all gone, forgotten in their final places of rest. These were people like the living, like us; people, who no longer have the opportunity to make the difference we now have opportunity to make in South Africa.

If the dead can see or wake up from their place of eternal sleep, they will be glad with so much enthusiasm to make the difference we now seek in the life of South Africa. They will be prepared to give all their earthly belongings to South Africa and go back to their eternal place of rest glad and fulfilled that they have done great good for humanity.

Weep not for the dead but for yourself, and repent for all the evils you have done in the land of your ancestors. Repent knowing that today you have a chance to make a great difference in the life of South Africa, but tomorrow may be no more.

Live not in South Africa like a silent lamb. Wake up from slumber and take stock of the future of South Africa for the common good of future generations. As a South African, take stock of your duties and obligations to this nation. The time is now to become part of history.

Take active participation in community development, in politics, in economic growth and development, and in uniting everyone together as one big happy rainbow family. No one can do it for you, only you can make this happen. The time is nigh.

We must not wait aimlessly and helplessly in our days right here in South Africa and let things continue the way they are before making this important vital decision in our life. We must not say, "Let's leave the black people to run things and lets' mess up our country together." We must not wait to die before wishing we could have done our country proud and great.

This is the kind of truth and reality that should rule our minds and occupy our hearts as we make efforts to create a turnaround in the fortunes of this great nation. We can run from the reality of life, hide or bury the truth, shy away from sacrifice, and inherit the earth. But we cannot run or shy away from our real future, which lies is the dark dept of mother earth. We cannot run away from ourselves, or from the shadows of death. We cannot hide

or run away from South Africa. We cannot escape from the future of South Africa. Even if we try to hide and run now, the future of South Africa will not escape our children and future generations.

The real future we crave for and cry about lies in the solitary confined space of a grave. This is why the undertaker industry is a booming industry, an industry that is thriving and successful. It is an industry that will never fail or die.

A clothing business or car business can fold up due to lack of clients. Big banks and multinational industries and corporations can be liquidated, and world economies can go into recession, but the undertaker business can never lack clients. People must die as nature dictates life. Good deeds will never die.

The young shall grow, and the old shall die. Accidents happen, and natural causes, sickness and deaths can take its toll on anyone, irrespective of age, race or colour. Natural disasters can strike anyone at any time. This is why we have to make meaningful sacrifices now, right now, and contribute everything we have within our power, and give all that we are to make a difference in the lives of the great people of South Africa.

As a people, we are all one, same human beings, having the same gift of life, and deserve the same better life in our limited days on earth. That is how to be fair to each other. By being fair to each other, we will be glad to have a peaceful life and coexistence. So make a difference now in the life of South Africa, a contribution to the life of society, and to the future of your generations.

Joe Odiboh

Chapter 10
The Unfinished Business

There is need for true integration process, the need to correct the social and economic imbalance of the past, and the need to reflect on the past, in other to address the current problems which today impact on the lives of the people of this great nation. This of course is the unfinished business of freedom and democracy in the lives of all South Africans.

There is the unfinished business of lack of unity in diversity, total lack of morality and moral values not only as individuals, but also as communities and society.

This lack of morality and moral values have destroyed in one way or the other the moral fabric of the society, and the very moral foundation upon which true freedom and democracy for all is founded by the founding fathers of freedom, peace, truth and justice.

Today in South Africa, love is expensive and hatred is cheap, and true integration process is far from realization. Most of the coloureds, Indians, white and black people live far apart in their various communities, and making South Africa more divided as it was in the days of apartheid regime. All these hatred and racial bias and divisions are possible due to lack of morality and moral values in the hearts of men and women of this great nation.

This lack of togetherness and love reflects in the entire spectrum of our national life. This imbalance in society, have derailed the spirit of "Ubuntu"; that is the spirit of togetherness and love. It is the spirit of accepting each other as one big family and endeavour to do unto others as you would wish others to do unto you.

What we need in our society is the spirit of acceptance, tolerance and of giving and sharing something good in common for the betterment of our nation. That is the kind of spirit that 'Ubuntu' profess in the lives of all South Africans.

Practicing how to live this good idea is quite different from living it. However, people in this country do not practice what they preach, many do not care to preach this ideal anymore, nor do they live it as a moral obligation to each other in the society. Instead, people are beginning to preach the gospel of hatred, crime and violence.

All these hatred and violence in society are due to the hatred which inhabit the hearts of men, making people act like vampires in search of each other's blood to suck and lick out in the anger that have taken hold of their hearts and minds.

This unnecessary anger can be seen in parliamentary debates, in political campaigns and elections, in the social life, and in commerce and industry. It is noticeable even in arts and theatre, and reflects in the police service and judicial system.

The real issue is the big problem of how to unify all South Africans to live together as one community, and live side by side as neighbours, united economically with equal share of the nation's wealth and resources. People must learn to interact together socially without regards to colour or race, and take part in active politics without bias, gender, colour or race.

People must enjoy the same rights and privileges, ensuring that no colour, race or creed is better than the other, equality for all in all facets of their national life, and that no form of social, economic, and political domination creates a divide between citizens of the same nation.

This is a business that has to be finished in other to have true freedom and democracy for all in South Africa. In doing so, there will be true integration process, the spirit of togetherness and love will be fully restored, and all these will impact on the political future, safety and security of lives and properties. It will help reduce the incidence of crime, hate and violent attacks, and the future of all South Africans will be fully secured and safely guaranteed.

However beautifully said these things might seem, it is easier said than done. We all know that most human beings are wolves in human skin, the powers of the forces of evil in society, and that most people in life do not wish their neighbours and relations to find true joy and happiness in life. Some people always work day and night to pull down the ladders with which they were helped to climb to the top, making sure no one ever gets the opportunity to climb up those ladders of success and have a better life.

This is why such people like **Winfrey Oprah of the United States** have proven in life the need for raising hopes and dreams of other people far away in her singular selfless efforts to prove this theory wrong. **She built a school for girls in South Africa in her show of togetherness and love,** and she has set a pace for all South Africans and visitors to the land to follow. **She has single handily raised up a ladder with which the daughters of South Africa must rise and aspire to greater heights in life, something for which history and posterity will justify her name.**

There were others who wished to be worshipped forever by their friends and relations, ensuring that they stay alone and remained in the heart of success. They wish others to bow down to them and worship them like gods for their accomplishments in life, making sure that those who bow to them and worship them continue to bow their heads and remain in poverty forever.

These are the people who wish most black and coloured South Africans to remain in their poor settlements and poor conditions of life forever so that they can serve as servants, messengers, nannies, domestic workers, mine workers, cleaners, gardeners, and farm workers without a voice in society.

These kinds of retrogressive forces in society are the enemies of progress in South Africa. They are the kind of people who think that domestic workers, miners, and cleaners have no right to decent wages, decent homes, decent standard of living, good cars, and no right to train their children to become doctors, engineers and scientists.

These evil forces do not wish people in the poor informal settlements and the vast majority of the unemployed people to find a means of livelihood, or have access to the good things of life in South Africa. This is not only an issue of race, colour or nationality, it is an issue of the kind of people some people are in life, the wickedness of their spirit, the nakedness of their evil hearts, the dirt and filth in which their body and soul is composed, and which gives them the pleasure and joy to see others living in dirt and filth.

It is only people who are dirty and filthy at heart that will for so long enjoy the pleasures of seeing other people living in poverty, dirt and filth in these informal settlements, or under poor conditions of life all over South Africa, and without doing anything meaningful to help stop this circle of poverty, dirt and filth in the lives of the people.

The government of ANC is doing so much, but it needs help, and I believe every single white South African, and everyone has a role to play to make South Africa great and stop the circle of poverty, dirt and filth in our lives.

This brings to mind our moral obligations to the society in the spirit of Ubuntu. This spirit is a living spirit which must dwell in the hearts of the great men and women of this great nation. This is where we have to think about what is right or wrong in our lives.

The question about right or wrong comes into play in issues like this. It brings into mind what certain values some races want and what others want. How to bridge this gap is another issue of national debate and moral principles.

The onus of this debate and moral principles hinges on the facts that there is freedom and democracy, and the black people are in power. How this power is used like their white counterparts of the past apartheid regime to empower the black people to have the same social and economic conditions of life as equals with the white people, is the fundamental question that needs positive answers and dynamic approach to end the inequality in society.

The government has a responsibility to its entire people and should borrow a leaf from progressive nations to ensure that no black South African deserves to live in shacks or feed from the dustbin or rubbish dumps. This is exactly what the government is struggling to do without help or cooperation from most of its citizens or multinational corporations and businesses.

One way they can do this is to ensure a very strong and productive social welfare system like it is in the case of Ireland. There is no other way. Ireland is a model. This is the solution to South African problem of poverty, poor standard of living, medical cards issues and health facilities, and putting an end to inequality and the problems of crime and violence.

The content and standard of a social welfare system is what determines the strength of a nation, the quality of life, and the quality and strength of their basic standard of living.

South African government should model the Irish social welfare service system in content and quality. The issue of qualitative services is very important in this program of action. The quality of this social welfare service will determine the quality of life of every South African, and make the issue of unemployment and crime a non-issue.

No-matter what we do or try to avoid this great sense of responsibility to the people of this great nation, there is no way out of poverty and social inequality and injustice in this country without a viable social welfare system.

In Ireland for example, it is very difficult to see a cop carrying a gun. Most regular cops do not carry guns, and the presence of guns in the society is very rare. Those who fight violent crimes are special task forces whose presence can hardly be noticed, because of the low incidence of crime in the Irish society and due to effective police system.

This is made possible because of the quality of social welfare services in that country which guarantees every Irish citizen or immigrants a qualitative basic standard of living, ensuring the provision of basic human needs, social equality, and justice for all.

In this kind of system, everyone can afford the basic needs of life which includes decent housing, food, clothing, and basic expenses, including access to good health, where everyone has a GP appointed by government to look after health needs in cooperation with the hospitals.

This is what is called freedom and democracy, equal rights and justice. This is what the government of South Africa must do for its entire people with the resources of the state, the gold, tax incomes, diamonds, platinum, land, tourism, and everything that bring income revenue to government of the people, for the people and by the people. If this is done, such people or legends like Nelson Mandela, Oliver Thambo, Walter Sisulu, Steve Biko, Joe Slovo, and many others will find peace and rest, knowing that it is now well with all South Africans.

The resources of the state is more than enough to do this, same way as the apartheid regime did it for the white people with the same resources which is now in the hands of government. South African leaders and government should not see themselves as black government, but as South African government for all the people. The money is there, the manpower is there, and the human and natural resources is more than available to achieve this aim and objectives.

Once the white people and the investors see that the government can be trusted, and they are not there to corrupt themselves but to ensure social services that guarantee good standard of living for all South Africans, the hate and greed in human hearts will fade away, racial bias will wither into the thin air, and everyone will be encouraged to invest and contribute without let or hindrance to the good of society.

A wonderful social welfare service system does not discourage capital investment and growth; it only enhances and ensures that there is enough for everyone to aspire to greater heights in life. It is the key or salvation to all the major problems that confront all South Africans, and has impeded the common bonds that unite the people.

Socialism is a moral issue while capitalism is capital punishment for some people and capital greed for others. Capitalism is the root of all evils in society, the cause of all hate and violence, and it is the weapon used by Satan to destroy mankind by our insatiable human desires. Capitalism is like crack cocaine, one of the most dangerous drugs used by Satan to make life unbearable for mankind.

It is what leads to poverty, marginalization, corruption, abuse, injustice, racism, crime and violence. It creates jealousy, rebellion and genocide. It does not ensure equal rights and justice. Above all, any capital investment or wealth of a nation can crash into a bottomless pit in a few seconds.

Even the best bank in the world can lose all its funds in a twinkle of an eye through improper trading. Too many things can go wrong in a capitalist world because it is the businesses of dog eat dog. Hence today, the world is going through a period of global recession without asking ourselves the question, 'Why? Where did our money go to? Did it go out of the earth to enrich other planets and aliens?

While capital is a necessity in business, how the capital is used to better the lives of the people is what makes capital an important factor in human lives. God have in his mercy and grace created the land, which is perfect and rich enough in all its glory to provide for all the people on earth.

The land helps to yield the resources used for the good of society. It is big enough to provide us with enough food, shelter, and everything we need on earth. If there is no air, land and water, there will be no human life on earth. It is so sad that only the minority of people on earth use these resources of the earth for their own selfish interest and human greed, while others are suffering and smiling. This is what makes capitalism and human greed go hand in hand with the pleasures and satisfaction of the devil, who is the king of capital punishment.

Those who find joy and satisfaction in inequality and injustice are the messengers and agents of Satan. It is for South Africans to review this issue, and decide what side they are on, the part of equal rights and justice, or the part to hell. The part to hell in South Africa is the part that consumed such innocent great talented musicians like Brenda Fasi, caught in the circle of capitalism and drugs, drugged to death; and Lucky Dube, caught in the circle of crime and violence, robbed and killed in cold blood by criminal elements in our society.

Capitalism is so destructive and evil, that it requires some socialism and social structures and institutions to check and balance its influence on society. This is exactly what the Irish people have done by providing for its entire people through social welfare services in the face of capitalist government in search of investments and prospects to grow the economy.

Ireland has not allowed the recession it is in and European economic crises to stop it from being there for the people. In fact, the country has unwound its way out of the bailout. This is what makes this country very special in Europe, the inner strength it has in ensuring that the government is not about capital, but about the people and inhabitants in that land. It is this ideal and virtues, its moral obligations to its people, the commitment and sincerity of purpose to serve its people that make Ireland a success in overcoming most of all its problems. This is the spirit of 'Ubuntu' in the Irish society.

Though all nations have their problems, what is important is service delivery to the people. Problems will always be there in life as a way of life, but every human life does not exist forever. So as human beings, and as government, we must always remind ourselves about the relative important of human life, and convince our hearts that nothing on earth is more important and valuable than every single human life, and try to protect this life, and ensure that it is a life well lived on earth.

This should be the priority of every government on earth. This should be the motto of government in providing for all its citizens. This is what the government in South Africa should do to insure the future of that country if ANC must continue to have meaning in the lives of the electorates. The ANC must know right now that it is not a political party that will last forever. This is why it is necessary to act right now and make South Africa a better place to live.

While there is inequality in society, there is lack of effective social welfare services and service delivery. Whatever social services and service delivery that are available, it need to be reprogrammed and re-planned in such a way as to add value and quality of life to the living conditions of all South Africans. It should be a program of action sponsored by government, businesses, investors, and tax reforms.

Government is not simply about ensuring better lives for all those in government like the masters in the book "Animal Farm", who are entitled to fresh milk, while others must toil and labour in vain only to die in pain, poverty and misery. It is about providing for everyone in a way that ensures equality and justice in the spirit of 'Ubuntu'.

Equality and justice is what brings peace and cohesion and reduces the incidence of crime and violence, as well as protests and rebellion in society. It is what makes people to see each other as equals and as human beings and help reduce the incidence of race hate and racial bias in a country such as South Africa with all its dynamics, culture and languages. It is a unifying factor that can heal the racial wounds in this great nation, and bring about human respect and dignity of life.

Going to Ireland have exposed me to what is called fundamental human rights, true freedom and democracy. It has exposed me to what it means to have a basic standard of living for its citizens and visitors to the land. It has exposed me to the great difference between Ireland and most of the rest countries of the world. It has shown me what the spirit of 'Ubuntu' is. In Ireland, I have seen what is called real and just police service, and real judicial system.

It has enlightened me in the understanding of what it is for the government to guarantee basic human needs for all its people and immigrants to the land. It has opened my eyes to the reality and existence of human rights and justice for all, irrespective of colour, race and creed. It has proved that whether or not the people were racist or biased, it has no effect or meaning to human growth and development. Everyone is guaranteed a better life, freedom and justice.

While the pro-democracy government in South Africa seem to try to emulate this system in Ireland, it has not provided for the black people adequately the way the apartheid government provided for its own people. Injustice and gross human rights violations still prevails, and human dignity have not been fully restored.

The freedom fought for and won have not been fully realized, and this is one reason for violent protests because fundamental human rights have not been inclusive of basic standards of living and freedom to live peacefully without crime and violence as one South Africa free from oppression and repression of the past as a democratic republic.

When the late former President Nelson Mandela was voted into power as the first democratically elected president in 1994, every South African was very hopeful and believed that South Africa was finally free, and that the imbalance and social injustice of the past will be fully redressed in every facet of their national life. Nelson Mandela played the role of the father of the nation and did his utmost best to unite all South Africans together as one people, with one hope, one nation, and one destiny.

The African National Congress, (ANC) which is the ruling majority party have meaningful programs and agendas to redress this imbalance, but as time gone by, there seem to be divisiveness further and further, lack of focus, and without efforts being made for proper integration process that guarantees true freedom and democracy for all. The political infighting in the various political parties, killing each other, murders and assassinations, lack of respect and discipline, and with new leaderships, seem to downplay the meaning of true freedom and democracy.

The lack of accountability to the people, politics of bitterness and hate, racial bias, and corruption, which had reared its ugly head, have in one way or the other derailed the meaningful plans, programs and agendas meant to remedy the injustice of the past and create a united front in nation building. Some of these problems are moral issues that require moral solutions to the problems of moral degradation in the entire political spectrum and national life of society.

Though the efforts of government cannot be underestimated, or underrated, it is important to note that the government have made great achievement and taken great strides to mend fences. The modalities for service delivery, frauds and corruption which remain unchecked have made this work and efforts harder in a rational point of view. This is because every effort being made by government is brought backwards by the attitude of some interest groups and some reactionary forces in the society, including the high rate of crime.

Above all, most South Africans as a people have not truly appreciated the efforts of government, and made no meaningful contribution to ensure true freedom and democracy for all. Most of these people, believe that freedom and democracy is freedom of madness to be rude and do anything they like, be it good or bad, moral or immoral.

They see it as freedom to insult and abuse anyone, freedom to disrespect the elders and people in government, freedom to smoke and drug themselves to death, freedom of alcohol abuse and abusive sex, freedom of unruly behaviour, and freedom to rape, kill or maim innocent children and babies.

This they see as the freedom to own everything free without having to work and earn a living, freedom to disassociate themselves from other people and create racial divide, and freedom to rob and kill their neighbours or foreigners. This is how some people interpret, or perceive their freedom to protest and demonstrate violently and destroy government services, infrastructures and facilities.

Freedom and democracy in South Africa have been wrongly interpreted, wrongfully managed, and wrongly adopted both in the government circle and in the lives of most South Africans due to ignorance, misinformation and lack of good ideals in public relations.

South Africans have various views and opinions about freedom and democracy and each individual interpret and execute these freedoms in their various ways and means in virtually nearly everything they do, think, or say in every facet of their national life, both as individuals, and in the public and private sectors of the economy.

All these kinds of ambiguous freedoms have further created confusion, racial bias and threaten to tear apart the very moral foundation and principles of the constitution, freedom and democracy, as well as the rule of law. The government, seem to take very lenient stand on crime and violence knowing the injustice of the past cannot be replaced with tyranny. The government is sympathetic with its people because for too long they were wrongly punished and marginalized.

These are some of the problems society has to contend with in their search for peace, freedom and democracy for all, without seemingly seen to worsen the situation by enforcing tough laws and using the resources of the state to punish offenders. Who are these offenders? The answer is obviously mostly the black and coloured people.

If the government should try to use tough laws and draconic means to discipline its citizens, or punish offenders, it would lose its popularity and political mandate, and bring about further protests and violence which could lead to political instability, chaos and anarchy.

Such a government would be seen to be authoritarian and South Africans are no longer ready for any tyranny, nor would they ever tolerate it. In fact, they will topple the leader or President of such a government through palace coup, and recall him. This goes a long way to show how complex and dangerous this situation is in South Africa forcing the government to maintain a liberal attitude towards its citizens for national peace and stability.

In a more polarized society such as the United States, they cannot tolerate the kind of freedom and democracy that exist in South Africa where most people interpret and execute their freedoms without regards to race problems or rule of law. It cannot tolerate people following their own set of rules or moral codes without regards to the constitution of the state, which bind everyone together as one. In other to uphold the ideals of society and the constitution, correctional facilities have become the country home for such offenders and unruly characters that seek to execute or create their own sets of freedom or rules in the United States.

Unlike America, South Africa is not fully integrated as one country, and does not have the full mandate of society from all sectors of the economy and from the various races to shape its citizens towards same ideals as one people knowing that the imbalance of the past have not been fully redressed to ensure or reflect one nation and one destiny.

With freedom and democracy, come responsibility and civic duties and obligations to the nation, as well as patriotism. Most South Africans have not been taught their civic duties and obligations, and many more are very ignorant about their rights and privileges.

Because of this ignorance, most of the people do not know what they should do to make a better South Africa, neither do they know the importance of civic duties and obligations, nor do they care about patriotism.

A nation that does not know or care about their civil rights, privileges and obligations to the state cannot become patriots and contribute meaningfully, constructively, and collectively and fight to uphold the ideals and virtues upon which the society is founded.

They do not even know the constitution or its ideals. I guess they only hear about the word 'Constitution' once in a while like a joke or swear word. This is because of lack of interest in nation building, ignorance and moral laxity in society with a low esteem.

There are no such programs these days for compulsory education and skills development, or compulsory community service, or compulsory youth service to the nation, even in the military. If every youth and all those committing heinous abominable crimes in South Africa are sent on compulsory military service to the nation, it will enlighten and educate them on their civic roles and obligations to their country, create integration process, and reduce the incidence of crime considerably.

This is something the government of post independence era, have not done. Instead they are busy with fighting among themselves in power tussle and over split milk. Youth leaders in the ANC have grown wings wishing they could fly above the sky so high like a hawk above the eagles. The youth wings wish they could be above the national body. This was the problem between the former and expelled youth leader of the ANC who is now his own party leader, Hon. Julius Malema and President Jacob Zuma in the ANC. Who is to blame? No one should blame Hon. Julius Malema. They should blame the existing system in South Africa with its own set of freedom and inequality in society. Many people are confused and apprehensive about the future and not knowing what road they should take. Malema has since been vindicated by the formation of his own political party which has become one of the top parties in South African political landscape.

Americans will die for their nation, and come together as one in time of trouble, united and strong to ensure that America survives as the greatest nation on earth. This is also one reason, why, the United States of America, have adopted the patriot act for all its citizens. This is why they all came together as one to elect the first black President Barrack Obama, as the 44th President of the United States of America.

This kind of ideals is missing in the South African context, knowing that the white people here in South Africa are not as open in mind like those in the US, nor are they ready to make sacrifices to ensure the survival and better life for all in South Africa, especially the thought of sharing their wealth or resources with the black people. This is because; most of them are still undermining and underrating the black people in society.

The best they can do for now as white people in their hearts for South Africa is to build a united front to defend their own minority interest and ensure that they will crush anyone or anything that threatens their investments, properties, and the safety and security of their lives and heritage.

The coloureds and the Indians will do the same for themselves, while the black people who do not have much stake or business interest in the economy will defend themselves against tyranny and oppression. This is not how it was suppose to be in one nation, because such thoughts and attitude is selfish, unproductive and unskilful. It is divisive and not of national interest.

In the midst of all these, the criminals and negative elements in the society, the enemies of progress, will be hoping and praying that in the event of national crises, they could loot and cause mayhem, arson, destruction of lives and properties, vandalize, and cause further chaos and anarchy.

The lazy rightists who are terribly biased and unforgiving, will be nursing in their hearts how they could act like the Zimbabweans and take back from the Indians, whites and coloureds communities, that, which they believe rightfully belongs to them as black people, and without thinking or caring about the implications and consequences of this mission impossible.

Many black people, especially those in the informal settlements believe they were already down to earth in their various locations and shacks in the ghettoes, so they have nothing to lose by being unpatriotic and chaotic. Many others believe any change in situation, be it chaotic or lawless was better than the present living conditions in these poor communities and they are not prepared to fight and die, or make sacrifices in the preservation of the white man's wealth, in the same country that has impoverished the black race.

Where then is freedom and democracy with civic rights, obligations and patriotism? This absence of patriotism is another fundamental problem, which the government find so hard to resolve, so difficult to enforce. Above all, ignorance and lack of unity in diversity makes the situation more complex and ridiculous. Even so, the government is aware of all these problems and they try to encourage people to learn their rights, privileges and civic obligations. The question is no-matter how difficult the government efforts are; how many people are ready to learn and change their mind-set?

The major problem in South Africa is not about education, ignorance and learning, but about mind-set, about personal ego, about individuality in the face of bitterness and racial divide. It is about the strange feelings and thoughts which creep up in their minds in the way they see and regard their country, and in the way they wish to live and die in it. This poor and difficult mindset is a negative influence in society.

All these have created a careless attitude towards what they can do for South Africa, and with a major focus on what they can gain from South Africa. Most black and coloured people have the belief that the white people have stolen so much and gained too much from South Africa, and it was their turn to do the same. This is the mindset of most people in South Africa, something everyone pretend to be ignorant of, something that has become a negative source of human influence and criminality in society.

Some South Africans, especially those from the coloured communities often boast that they will rather rob from the white people than to rob from their black brothers. Most black people also feel the same towards their coloured brothers. Even among the coloured communities, there is a great divide and discrimination with regards to shades of colour and hair texture.

They often discriminate among themselves and remain yet another divided community with identity conflicts. All these play prominent roles in their criminal activities and gang wars. The black people in a coloured family are regarded as the black sheep in the family. There, they have certain coloured people regarded as the green eyes, light-y, white-y, blond-y, long-y-hair, and love-y and so on.

Above all, the white people are targets in South Africa because they are not seen as comrades; the black and coloured people believe the white people took away their rights, the resources of the state, their wealth and their pride and human dignity. Many people think the white people of this nation are being selfish and uncaring to the needs of the people of this great nation.

They seem only to be there for themselves and their families, and that they are not working with the government to ensure a better tomorrow for all South Africans. This is how the vast majority of the people think about the white people.

Feelings and thoughts that are dangerous and cannot help anyone in this nation.

This is why the few criminal elements among them often target tourists, rob supermarkets, rob white vulnerable people with impunity on the streets and street corners, and also target white ladies to snatch their bags or mug them. A few black people who are criminals would rather prefer to rob from the supermarkets, and from their black brothers or foreign blacks or immigrants than white or coloured people.

They know if they dare try to rob coloured and white people, they might get shot or killed without remorse, and that will be that. They will simply die for nothing like dogs. The law will be on the side of the assailants, the white or coloured people. This is why the black criminals operate locally in black townships or in Johannesburg with lots of black people and immigrants.

However, the only thing, most black people actually need in South Africa is equal rights and justice, which includes rights to be like the white people in every way possible. This is all they have ever prayed for, it is all that they wished; true freedom and democracy, equal rights and justice to become one world in South Africa.

It is one world with better life for all, and not freedom to be poor in the various black settlements. This is the danger in South Africa, a country of two worlds that flow side by side in irony.

Joe Odiboh

Chapter 11
Taking Meaningful Risks

One way of overcoming this imbalance, and take profitable risks, is the task of every South African to take a chance and make meaningful contributions to correct the imbalance of the past and compliment government efforts. The white people can decide to wilfully empower the black people through education, commerce, employment, decent wages, training, skills acquisition, manpower development, and every way possible.

Every white person must fight day and night to see that no South African live in shacks or Wendy houses and far below the poverty line. Once the black and coloured people see every white person fighting for the rights of black people to earn a decent life and decent wages, the black people will appreciate the white people more than ever before.

This will bring about peaceful coexistence and make the white people not targets or enemies, but as comrades in progress. This risk of rationalizing the wealth of society is one great step that will bring about truth, peace, and justice in South Africa.

It is better to be compassionate and share what you have with the poor than to wait for the poor to fight to have a share of what you have. In waiting, the end may not be as honourable or pleasant as in being our brothers' keeper. This risk of compassion and sharing, is a noble risk, it is a risk for togetherness and love.

In this togetherness and love, it is the task of all South Africans to make sacrifices and advance themselves in risk taking. All South Africans must not be afraid to take risks in life that can raise the country to greater heights and glory.

These include the type of risks that can lead to individual and community growth and development and bring about the revenue necessary to better the lives of all South Africans that are lacking in patriotism. It involves the risk of taking steps of practising how to live together in harmony as one nation, one common goal, and one destiny.

It requires the risk of white and coloured people to join the ANC and make the ANC a rainbow party with equal rights of all races to participate in the party activities and set a pace in unification of the country and all its peoples through ideal leadership elected on merit and not in colour. The ANC should no longer be seen as a black man freedom party but as a national party composed of the majority of all races.

This includes the risk of making efforts to ensure a true and lasting integration process, free of racism, and practice the belief that all men and women were created equal, and with equal privileges, equal rights and justice in South Africa.

It also include the risk of rationalizing the wealth in society in a way that every South African have a fair share of what is in South Africa, and ensure a better life for all without regards to race.

Unless this is done, crime and violence will continue to prevail and become part of those aspects of life which today have held all South Africans captives in the land of their birth. By practicing various moral codes, ethical conducts, and obeying the rule of law, South Africans will be moving away and shy away from the injustice of the past in their part to peace, truth, justice, and freedom for all.

That it should be a long and lasting democratic order that ensures better life for all, safety and security of lives and properties. This practice of how to become better South Africans is sure to eliminate the incidence of violent crimes, and bring about peaceful co-existence.

We all know that the criminal elements in South Africa are mostly the negative risk takers in destroying the good image of South Africa, and are destroying the freedom and democracy all South Africans fought for over the years. They take risks in armed robbery, breaking and entry, murders, stealing, and all forms of abominable crimes and violence. They have taken the risk of destroying this nation.

Even some of them including some cops and ex-service men have become ATM bombers, and robs cash and assets armoured vehicles. Such is the mean and low class thoughts of their mindset which has turned them from heroes to villains.

"If you want to eat a cockroach, you should eat a fat and delicious one", perhaps a cricket will be good and juicy. So speaking, any South African who wish to take risk, should take a risk that will be of benefit to all South Africans and become a hero and a big success that becomes a lasting legacy in life.

It is not a good thing to do something to be ashamed of, but something to be very proud of in life which will lead the individual to greater heights and achievement with great rewards. It is often better to conquer your fear factors in other to achieve greatness in life.

It is a great shame and disgrace when little petty criminals and gangsters engage in their little petty shameful activities and get killed like dogs and buried like rats in shame and disgrace. Fearlessness should not be used for criminal activities, but for great things and noble cause in life. If you want to die, it is good to die for something good.

If you are not a coward, it is good to make attempts to climb the Table Mountain rather than hide in the street corner with a gun and knife in the pocket thinking you are a strong guy. You are nothing but a fearful felon, a common thief, petty killer and murderer of unarmed vulnerable people because you want to smoke drugs. Real men do great things in life.

Those who are not afraid of achievements, must never be afraid of failure in education, business, enterprise, industry, sports, recreation, science and technology, service delivery, arts, literature, theatre, and in entertainment. It is necessary to develop a positive attitude towards individual life and towards the life of the nation if the country must move forward towards a better tomorrow.

One way of conquering fear is to think of the hero inside of you, what you can do for yourself and for South Africa, what you do best in your community, your interest, your hopes and dreams, and you should work very hard through practice and ensure you fulfil your hopes and aspirations to make a great difference in your life, in the life of your community, and in the life of all South Africans.

That is how to take risks, give selfless service, and do something fulfilling like people who travel long distances to climb to the summits of mountains such as mountain Everest, or perish along the way as heroes in the part to greatness.

The road or part to achievement and success in life is usually not an anus open able with one palm. It requires strength and determination, hard work, and the quest to do something great. That is risk taking, the risks that will make South Africa great, and make better citizens of all South Africans.

Taking meaningful risks requires practice, moral codes and values, as well as obeying the rule of law in this process. It must be the kind of risks that conform to the moral norms in society, and not risks meant to hurt or harm other people.

This is the business of all South Africans, a task that must be done to observe moral codes, rules and regulations that can guarantee a better future for all South Africans.

These rules and regulations enjoin against killing and murders, taking what is not given or stealing, sexual misconduct, racial discrimination, false speech, robbery, xenophobic attacks, and use of intoxicating drink when driving or drugs use and abuse, including those vices that tear society apart.

When South Africans start to learn and follow moral codes in the society, like it is in Ireland, it will deeply affect their personal and social life. The fact that they have to have a change of heart and must willingly undertake to be good citizens rather than see the rule of law as a set of commandments wilfully imposed on them by government is likely to have a positive bearing upon their conscience and awareness.

Feeling of race and colour is a natural phenomena in human nature same with tribalism and ethnicity. It is not supposed to be a problem but a thing of human pride and dignity that unites various cultures, various colours and makes a country beautiful like the various colours in nature and in floral.

The variation in colours is what creates beauty and aesthetic values in human nature. Black and white is neutral or natural colours in art, and is used in light and shades of colours, or in colour toning. So, black people and white people are just one and the same, neutral and natural, who need each other in order to create a balance in peaceful coexistence for national growth and development.

Naturally, racial feelings can arise for people who are not yet free in their hearts and minds. Some white and coloured people in South Africa still cannot believe that all race and human being are equal, and thinking like this may not really help South Africa as a country.

This kind of negative feelings is a personal problem and not a national issue. How you feel about yourself is different from how people feel about you. It is better to feel good about yourself and let others feel good about themselves, and without making efforts to make other people feel bad about them-selves.

By feeling good about your-self, you must also feel good about other people so that everyone can feel good about the society and appreciate each other believing that together South Africa is blessed as a rainbow nation. The various races in South Africa is something of joy and national pride; it is something of strength and colour, which calls for a great celebration.

It is not a feeling that should frustrate each other but a feeling of appreciation. If you do not feel good about other races, you must find a way of dealing with that feelings and hate yourself for feeling that way. By hating yourself, you are dealing with reality, and knowing you cannot hate yourself the way you hate others, you will end up accepting the truth and loving yourself for appreciating the truth.

By appreciating the truth, you will be appreciating people of other races. Any feelings of frustration do not justify acting them out with someone outside of the same race. Therefore, one could argue for the benefit of freeing one's own mind which would relieve the frustration and prevent racial conflicts and bias.

While the value of family in raising children to believe that all human being are equal is essential, it is undisputed among most black South Africans who are the people who truly believe in equality and justice for all.

The black folks are the ones who appreciate the presence of white people more that the white people appreciate them. This is an undisputed fact in South Africa. The black people believe all human being are equal, and they are very receptive, understanding, and believe in peaceful coexistence with other people and other races in the land of their birth.

I know and believe that no country in Africa other than South Africa will allow them-selves under humiliation, to live with the white people the way they have done in this country, which rightfully belongs to the black people. This is why the white people in South Africa must respect and appreciate the black people because respect is a two-way compliment. One good turn deserves the other in other to live together peacefully.

It does not mean that people should not take pride in themselves and their race or colour. Taking pride in ones race is permitted as a way of preserving one's own dignity, culture and language, and can be practiced for a variety of reasons at the discretion of the community as a way of life. Race is about culture, beliefs, and the preservation of values in society.

It is about the culture and tradition of the people handed down from one generation to the other. This is consistent with the view that the purpose of racial behaviour between races and colour is not limited to feelings but necessary for unity in diversity. There is no law on earth which prohibit taking pride in ones colour or race.

Only a rare few people in South Africa are ready to fully handle the emotional side of racism as it affects them from day to day. As the saying goes, "it is easy to forgive, but difficult to forget", and it is intolerable to see some people continue to suffer the same fate in disguise.

Joe Odiboh

Chapter 12
The Healing Process

People must heal from within, and develop the spirit of racial cohesion. Imbibing the spirit of "Ubuntu", or patriotism, with the mindset of one nation, one destiny, and one people; is attempting healing from without and renewing one's own feelings and thoughts. Healing expresses truth and justice, freedom of the mind and self-exultation to be free and accepting.

Healing process is a very painful process of self discipline and determination to accept that which is unchangeable. It is painful at heart, it tears the heart apart, and it is full of doubt. It is like walking in a lonely difficult quiet part to self mortification. But it is honest and it leads in the right direction.

Truly harmonious and deeply satisfying relationships between people of various races are only available for people who have resolved their deepest internal conflicts. And until you have resolved your deepest personal conflicts, your job is to learn how to be in an ideal relationship with yourself. If you cannot relate with yourself as a South African, it is impossible for you to relate with people of other races, or unite together with other people to build a better South Africa.

Understanding is the first step to repentance. If you do not understand what really happened in South Africa, it is difficult to understand the need for sacrifice, tolerance, and the urgent need for peace, truth, and reconciliation. "It is easy to forgive, but difficult to forget, because an unforgotten mind, is an unforgiving heart."

Doing well in developing a nation does not mean other people must suffer and pay with their lives and stripped of their fundamental human rights. There is nothing any one can say or do to justify the apartheid policy of racial discrimination and segregation.

The only question is about our racial behaviours, how we are behaving badly as individuals in not making concrete efforts to put right all that is wrong in society by complimenting government efforts, and make efforts to have true integration process and unite together as one to make a better tomorrow.

Most South Africans seem to be afraid of speaking the truth and accepting it as part of the healing process. Some of them rejoice at false speech made by politicians to deceive them at elections and political rallies. Others speak falsely to further incite violence and racial tensions and cause chaos and anarchy in the country. This is what happens in most communities, something that must be stopped.

Abandoning harsh speech is necessary in overcoming the injustice of the past; in this way one employs speech which is blameless, pleasant, acceptable, heart-touching, civilized, and agreeable. Abandoning frivolous speech; one uses speech, which is appropriate to the occasion, correct, purposeful, and in accordance with the decency required of each other.

One utters words that are worthy, opportune, reasonable, meaningful, and straightforward. Such speeches show moral values, respect and love for one another in society. It ensures progress and respect for human life and dignity.

By avoiding falsehood, we learn to speak the truth about the state of affairs, and help bring about constant awareness and direct control of greed and avarice, which motivate wrong livelihood and one learns to develop generosity, altruism, and selfless service to society without hate or racial bias. By saying the truth, one is able to contribute to peace and reconciliation process and think of what is good and morally just for all South Africans.

However, in all human transactions such as in politics, commerce and industry, we seem to use other individuals for our own benefit and these transactions only become immoral when the utility of the transaction is one sided.

Killing a human being in South Africa, which has become a common feature, for instance, is not basically a human nature; if it were; human beings would have ceased to exist a long time ago. To practice how to be a better South African is thus to train in preserving one's true nature, not allowing it to be modified or overpowered by negative forces.

The social attitude of people towards each other in this country is worth lamenting, very abusive and racist due to moral degradation in society. We must not forget that on the social level in society, morality contributes to harmonious and peaceful coexistence among community members and consequently helps to promote social growth and development.

In a society where morality prevails and members are conscious of their roles, there will be general security, mutual trust, and close cooperation, these in turn lead to greater progress and prosperity.

Without morality there will be corruption and disturbance, and all members of society are adversely affected. Most of the problems that South Africa experiences today are connected, directly or indirectly, with a lack of good morality.

The constitution provides a wholesome foundation for personal and social growth. They are practical principles for a good life and the cultivation of virtues. If we understand the objectives of constitution and realize its benefits, we will see moral values as an integral part of life rather than as a burden that we are compelled to shoulder.

True moral values are not commandments imposed by force; they are a way of life undertaken in order to achieve a desired objective. We do not follow the rule of law to please other people, but for our own good and the good of society.

As individuals, we need to train to be better citizens and in our moral values both at home, in various communities, and in our religious worship and beliefs to lead a good and noble life. As good citizens, we need to help maintain peace and harmony in society and facilitate the progress of the common good of all South Africans.

It is therefore important that South Africans have to re-evaluate their moral codes and values to become better citizens, and make meaningful sacrifices to empower those who were less privileged and abused in the past by a system that have made them victims of their colours and race.

Though, South Africans are proud to have won true freedom and democracy, but political freedom is different from economic freedom, or freedom of association, and freedom to become better people in life. Freedom and democracy does not mean freedom of injustice and poverty.

It does not mean freedom to allow injustice in society to remain buried under the carpet in the name of democracy. Any attempt to think of life without the white people is like asking for the black clouds to hang over our heads from one generation to the other.

It is like asking to be like Zimbabwe. South Africa is our country, and we must not allow anyone to turn South Africa to Congo Brazzaville, DRC, Zimbabwe, Nigeria, Niger, Somalia,

Kenya, Uganda, Eritrea, Ethiopia, Guinea, Liberia, Ghana, or Ivory Coast. We cannot and must not allow anyone to drag South Africa to the mud.

Investment is very costly and expensive; the white people have invested their lives in South Africa. The black and coloured people must appreciate the government and understand also that government efforts require proper planning, and require a great deal of time to provide for everyone.

Rome was not built in one day. South Africans must develop the spirit of trusting their government and learn to respect leadership with togetherness and love. Everyone needs to help the government and be part of the transformation process.

The government cannot do everything alone in isolation. They need your help; they need you and me to help make meaningful investment in the life of South Africa in whatever way or form. Yes! We can! You too can be our leader. Yes! You can lead South Africa to a greater and better future. Yes! You can!

This is the spirit of "Ubuntu", the love of peace, the need for truth and the necessity for reconciliation. Every reasonable South African of any colour or creed knows this fact, and that is why they have humbled themselves, and have accepted peace, truth, and reconciliation, knowing that a house that divides against itself shall fall. It cannot stand the test of time.

That is why the ANC slogan is the voice and language of excellence, of hope, and of light to shine and lead all South Africans into a better tomorrow. "Together, we can build a better South Africa". Let that slogan, be your personal motto in life. Let it be the source of energy and motivation that drives everyone to contribute meaningfully to the common good of this great nation.

The maturity of South Africans in dealing with very complex situation shows that South Africans are the most reasonable and understanding people in the world. They are the most humane, respectable, responsible, and reasonable people on earth.

They are selfless, understanding, tolerant, perseverance, and are the most hospitable people imaginable under the sun. There is no doubt in my mind that the entire world, especially the white race owes the black South Africans a debt of gratitude, respect, contributions, and reparations to better the lives of the black communities.

It is also necessary for the white minority in South Africa, the business communities, financial institutions, and investors to respect the black people and make sacrifices to ensure that they prove to the black people that they appreciate their deep sense of understanding for accepting things the way they are in South Africa.

This is why the white minority, business, and investors should show signs of responsibility with common sense, and the understanding that it is good to contribute in every way possible, and make selfless sacrifices by assisting the government in service delivery program for all South African communities. The European Union have a great responsibility to the people of South Africa. The legacies of former President Nelson Mandela will heel all our hearts.

Chapter 13
RDP Housing Programs

There are so many beautiful properties everywhere in South Africa, mansions and empty sky-scrappers for the white people, but the vast majority of the black people cannot dwell in them. They can only serve as labourers, domestic workers, cleaners, and workers in those buildings. Sky-scrappers can be used by government as council houses and it will help end the circle of poverty and underdevelopment in the ghettoes or informal settlements.

There is fresh milk and honey but most black people can only drink sour milk "Amanzi" to fill their stomachs. Let us come together as one family and ensure we cater for the needs of one South African family. Living in sky-scrappers is better than the shacks in the locations or informal settlements.

Everything good in South Africa is tied up in investments that belong to the investors and their generations of children. Nearly everything belonged to the past, to the white people, and the oppressors. It is time to ensure that all things being equal, togetherness as one, united we stand together as one. Let there be no more visions of one race being oppressed by the other. Let there be nothing like minority or majority race. Let us have people of every colour or race coming together as one in South Africa to become the human race where excellence and merit reigns supreme.

The most painful aspect of everything is that, there are abundance of vast expanse of land everywhere in South Africa, farms, beautiful properties spread all across the nation, empty sky-scrappers all around the cities, yet, the poor black and coloured communities are crammed in little shacks cramped together in little houses and small flats in their locations.

While some people get big apartments and houses built but the government to help address their housing needs, some others get small RDP houses built with asbestos in replacement for some shacks in small plots of land, with barely, no room, for people to move or breathe.

We seem to forget that we are human beings and not flock of sheep and goats that must be grouped together in the field. The best place to build RDP houses is in the white suburbs so that the black and coloured communities can live together side by side with the white communities.

This is the spirit of true integration process. For too long, South African housing policies and institutions have segregated people into racial locations. It is no use going further to create black communities only for the black people, coloured communities only for the coloured people, and white communities only for the white people. This is not helping the integration process in South Africa, or helping in reducing anger, incidence of crime and violence.

The government must try to mix people together for better understanding and racial cohesion. The government must emulate the white settlers and provide also for the black and coloured people what the apartheid government created for their white settlers in the same format within the white communities.

This will create sanity in society and the black people will like to live among the white people in the same community as one people in one country. This is something the government has not promoted; instead they have further created more divide by not integrating the people among the white settlers and coloured communities. By doing this, they are ensuring that politics is played on racial line where black people will continue to have majority rule.

This is what late former President Nelson Mandela fought against. Nelson Mandela does not want any race to dominate another race whether in politics, economics, commerce or in industry. He wanted a South Africa with equal rights and justice. This is the right of every South African to become whatever he or she wanted to be in South Africa. Playing politics on racial line will never, never, and never produce the best leadership this country needs to move us forward to a greater tomorrow. The ANC must not take advantage of its glory as a freedom party to use the black people of this country for the leadership benefits of its members. South Africa belongs to all and leadership belongs to all South Africans.

The ANC must be in history and not in the present since the exit of Nelson Mandela. There is an urgent need for political reforms in the formation of Nation Republican Party and the National Democratic Party where every South Africa can belong to any of these two political parties, not as a white man or black man party. Both parties must belong to all South Africans of every race, colour, or religious affiliation. Both parties must have nothing to do with colour or race. It must have nothing to do with the past. This is the greatest step to real integration process and good leadership in this country. People must join both political parties on equal terms, and not in terms of the struggle. This is why the government must stop building houses for certain race in certain locations or settlements. They must build houses for all South Africans in mixed communities. The important thing must be the task of ensuring that no single South African is without a decent home.

The rooms in some RDP houses built only for the black and coloured communities are like squalors, unable to accommodate most large African families, where heat or cold, lack of food, poor sanitation, poor toilet system, hunger and unemployment have further aggravated their pains, forcing people into crimes and any means of livelihood, thus encouraging child abuse, homelessness, rape, and prostitution.

When people are parked together in a place like sardines, there are conflicts of interest, arguments, jealousy, and criminality that are unavoidable. In this situation, everyone sees what everyone does; no privacy; and hear what everyone says, and sees what everyone eats, smokes and drinks, which constitutes a bad influence in society.

When one person whispers, "Poor Service Delivery," everyone echoes "Poor Service Delivery," like flocks of birds in the trees and takes to the street for protest marches, destroying the future of South Africa, without even reasoning what constitutes poor service delivery, progress made by government, or it's limitations.

People who need service delivery in their locations must be reasonable enough to know that you cannot ask for service by destroying existing services. The finance and resources that would have been used for new services to these communities will have to be used to reconstruct the ones destroyed and vandalized during protest demonstration for service delivery.

This illustrates the danger in parking people and houses together in little spaces and little rooms. It kills the spirit of reasoning and imaginative composition. It makes people to be competitive in negative acts and deeds without proper thinking or time for effective reasoning. It degrades the standard of living in those communities.

The white settlers do not live like this, and they do not destroy the services, legacies and lasting monuments in their communities provided for them by the government. This is the reason why they move away from any area inhabited by black and coloured settlers. They do not wish to belong to the chaos and anarchy in these poor communities.

Even the coloured communities do not behave the way the black people behaves in their communities except that the coloured communities are too much into drugs and gangs wars. They do not destroy government infrastructures and properties, or government services in their communities. Only a few of them are involved in vandalizing properties because they are the lazy jobless people who consume alcohol and drugs as a means to end their lives and frustrate members of their communities by stealing and muggings. These are the ones who carry guns and knives in their pockets day and night.

The coloured people use the facilities in their communities effectively and maintain them for the good of their people. The poor state of life in the black communities is the cause of xenophobia, because, when one person drinks beer, and smokes dagga, saying, "Kweri-kweri", meaning 'foreigners'; others who are sober, or also drunk, join unconsciously in chanting this slogan, and takes to the street, killing innocent foreigners, looting, burning their shops and houses in jealousy and frustration. I pity the Zimbabweans and especially the Somalis who mostly live among them and open shops in those informal settlements and remote areas.

The black people do not call the white and coloured people 'Kweri-kweri', or the Indians, Chinese, Pakistanis, or anyone with a coloured skin. All these people are highly respected by the black people who regard them as fellow South Africans. There are no white or coloured refugees in South Africa. No person with a light skin is regarded and treated like illegal immigrants in South Africa, except their black African brothers and sisters. This is very unfortunate.

These coloured immigrants and white people are given residency by the Department of Home Affairs and treated with respect. Only fellow Africans people are the new wave of victims of hate and discrimination by most South Africans and the Department of Home Affairs.

Some black South Africans seem to hate black Africans from other African nations, calling their fellow black brothers from Zimbabwe, and their neighbours from Africa, 'foreigners' in an Africa country such as South Africa.

This shows that there is no room for positive thinking, or reasoning, because of poor living conditions of life in the various locations due to lack of proper integration process. When the white people and people from other nations see what the black people of South Africa are doing to other black immigrants in South Africa, they start to fear for their lives too.

They begin to wonder about their own security and safety. They start to see us like the Hutus and the Tutsis. This is not a good picture to paint of black people in South Africa before the rest of the world. All these are possible because of poverty and frustration that exist in the lives of the African people. The family bond in a home necessary for good parental upbringing is also lacking and missing in most shacks or little houses.

There is no room for positive thinking and sober reflection. This lack of space in the locations is the root cause of alcohol abuse in most families, sex abuse, worsened by drugs and prostitution. This is why a grandparent will share a stick of cigarette with a grandson, and granddaughter. Anyone can sleep with anyone. Step fathers often sleep with their step daughters and make babies in the process. Uncles sleep with their nieces and brothers sleep with their sisters.

Fathers share beer with their sons, and mothers share a glass of wine with their daughters, because they are used to sharing little space, little beds, and little chairs together, sharing all kinds of smoke, and not knowing the meaning of a taboo or privacy.

They do not know what constitutes an abomination, or strict principles and self - respect. To those in the coloured communities, everything is "lekker" or nice "It is deadlock," some of them would say. Most people use swears words in the front of their children without considering the negative impact of these swear words in child development. This is a very sad development in setting standards for communal growth and development in the coloured communities. Some fathers often sleep with their daughters. That is why in nearly every mouth you hear the swear word, 'Mansa... ...p...ssssss'.

During the days of apartheid, the white people ensured that they built the country for themselves with nice houses, enough spaces between houses, and made sure that they gave to themselves the very best of what life can offer them in South Africa. They knew exactly the kind of life good for the white race, and they gave it to themselves. They built South Africa for themselves like Europe, and pushed the other races aside.

It is important that the black people should look at the way the whites provided for themselves, what they provided for themselves, why they provided for themselves that way, and borrow a leaf from that kind of knowledge in providing same equal opportunities and better conditions of life for the black majority, and compete in bringing about equal rights and justice in the kinds of RDP houses, business, and employment with decent wages.

The more RDP houses being built by the government the more shacks and Wendy houses being set up in various places and locations. This is because these houses cannot house families comfortably. There are not enough rooms in them to accommodate members of the extended family. Politicians building RDP houses must take into account that the white people have small families, but the African traditional system encourages large family system and extended families.

It is no use shouting and preaching the gospel of "Ubuntu" when we cannot come together as one to provide for the common man. We can conquer crime and poverty by learning from the ways of the apartheid regime in the ways they provided everything in South Africa for the white race. It is no use being jealous or envious of the white people, we should try to create for ourselves what they created for themselves.

If the apartheid government can use the resources of this land for their own benefit, it is no use the ANC government keeps talking about BEE, Black Economic Empowerment without making it happen to every black man. The apartheid regime did not preach any gospel of WEE for White Economic Empowerment, before empowering the white race. What is good for the Castle Lager Beer is also good for the Carling Black Label Beer.

This is why former President Thabo Mbeki, categorized South Africa as two worlds. As a weeping President, he did his best for the people? Whether his best was good enough for the people is something only history will judge. However, what he said is very true because he is a very wise man who truly understands the cross he had to bear as a South African President during his reign.

He was a great and wise African leader who understood his powers and its limitations in other to create a balance between white and black people of South Africa. The onus, rest on how we wish to merge into one as black and white people in the way we administer our government.

If we are confused, we should set aside politics and go to the white people and beg them to teach us the secret of a better life and how to make good things happen for the black people in South Africa and for all South Africans. We should beg them to teach us the secrets of good service delivery, and good governance. We should beg them to lead us.

We should swallow our pride and go on our knees and beg Britain, Europe and Americans to teach us the secret of good governance, economic and social policies that can guarantee our people the kind of life being lived in some parts of Europe and Australia, especially regarding better standard of living.

There is nothing to learn from our fellow African nations, because the living conditions in those countries are pathetic and worth lamenting. They are bad examples for any progressive nation. They are bad news to the sore ears. They are problems to the rest of the continent. Most African leadership have shamed us as Africans.

While we try to maintain to the fullest the infrastructures and economics inherited from the apartheid regime, we must not forget to maintain our people. While we are reconstructing bridges, train stations, and roads, we must also try and reconstruct the lives of the black people in the way the government inherited them from the apartheid regime.

We must try and place much premium on the importance of the life of every single South African, and guarantee them social security, and basic standard of living, as it is done in the civilized world.

It is not compulsory that a black South African must suffer, and remain poor, because the black people in other African nations are suffering and impoverished. Let us now for once try and make a big difference and show other African nations what it is to be black and proud.

Until this is done, so that the black race and the coloured communities can have a share from the national cake, the freedom, equal rights and justice that we preach, is non-existent. What the black people do not need is freedom to be poor, suffering and smiling, like most of our counterparts in other African nations.

The white people, business, and investors should help the government to build at least decent houses close to their houses for their labourers, servants, cleaners, stewards, and domestic workers. In that way, a black South African will not be destined to live only in the black settlements, or ghettoes.

This is why common sense is necessary in helping the black South Africans fulfil their dreams, hopes, and aspirations in life, so that a balance is created between the rich and the poor. What the white people can do today as proof of their love for South Africa, will encourage other races to embrace each other as one nation and do likewise.

All these are possible because, South Africans have a great deal of humility and service to all mankind, the love of life, kind and law abiding. They are very understanding and selfless in their desire to help their neighbours. This desire is so strong that they often forget about their own interest and welfare.

The main reason why people vote at elections in South Africa, especially for the ANC, is because they do not wish to go back to bad dreams. The dreams of what apartheid did to them. They know that with the ANC, there is hope, and together we can build a better South Africa.

ANC have tried to prove that the interest of the common man is their utmost priority, even in the face of financial disability or constraint. This party is trying to do something for the people with their meagre resources. They have obstacles on their way because they have not fully embraced the white and coloured minority groups to become part of the leadership of the ANC. What is saving the government are existing structures and systems which run independently on its own, with or without the political will.

The government depends mostly on tax and a few other means to meet the needs of the people. The government have got no elaborate investments, no properties, no land, no farms, and no finance, because all these belonged long ago to the white people who own the land, the farms, the properties and all the companies, investments, and businesses that made South Africa what we see it to be today.

In the eyes of the world and visitors to South Africa, everyone acknowledges that South Africa is a beautiful and highly developed nation, free and fair in all that they do. Truly speaking, South Africans are simple people and very understanding and humble.

They are down to earth and do not know how to pretend or deceive others. They are the kind of people who accept and take life as it comes and goes. They are not greedy people and do not know how to cry for what they cannot have.

Because of this uprightness and a deep sense of humility, they have left the wealth and the good things of life as it is to the white people to enjoy in their land, while they encourage and invite the rest of the world to come to their land and enjoy that which they could not have.

They provide excellent hospitality to tourists and visitors, while they are suffering, smiling, and proud of their land the way it has come to be. This is the dynamics of the South African virtues.

They are not interested in millions or billions of hard cash to corrupt their ego; what they want is freedom, peace, truth and reconciliation. They needed a very good standard of living and a better life with decent wages.

If they could trust the DA, or a white minority party to give them freedom, justice, and a better life, good service delivery, the black and poor South Africans will vote for the white minority party and bring it to power. They will do this the same way the Americans brought President Barrack Obama to power in the United States.

Black South Africans are not racist people; they do not care where people came from, or the colour of any skin. They are not stupid people, knowing that there is no party or anyone in

South Africa whom they can truly trust, and who can deliver better than the ANC at the moment.

They know that the white people can never love the black people of South Africa the way they love themselves. They have learnt that experience is the best teacher. They know that the white South Africans will smile at you when they want to use you, then they turnaround and swear at you, thinking you are stupid and dumb.

As white people, apartheid have taught some of them and fashioned them with hate against their fellow South Africans. Many of them are two-face. Many of them can pretend to love you and smile at you while in their hearts they are mocking you and wishing you dead. Even so, they still seem to appreciate foreigners from other African nations more than our black brothers and sisters.

The incidence of xenophobia that occurred not too long ago is not something South Africans were proud of, or wished to happen. It was an unholy incidence of an action carried out by some group of frustrated and idle people, who do not represent South Africans as a people. These are people who can do worse things during demonstrations for poor service delivery against the government that provides for them.

I guess people simply overreacted and the problem spurred out of control because of anger and frustration caused by poverty and poor service delivery. A hungry frustrated man is an angry man. On the same note, foreigners should also know that when they are in another man's country, they should do things with common sense and self control, and try as much as possible to respect the owners of the land.

They must also learn to build mutual trust and respect for better relationship, and better understanding. It is not true that the black South Africans do not like their black foreign brothers and sisters. It is absolutely true that how an immigrant relates and live with the community that defines the relationship between foreigners and inhabitants of the land.

We must learn to love and appreciate each other and sympathize with each other in whatever way and by every means as black people. We must understand that we are all brothers of the same sword with common bonds that bind us together.

Government have made great efforts to ensure that every South African own a house in their development program within a set time and date, and have taken great pain and done great in building houses for the vast majority of its citizens, especially for the black people and some coloured communities.

Not much is done for the white people in this regard, because they are seen not to have housing problems, and they already own all the decent houses in South Africa. While most South Africans are very appreciative to the government, so many others who have not yet got their houses are complaining bitterly day or night, demonizing the government and crying wolf where there is no wolf.

These people expect the government to build houses for everyone overnight without appreciating the efforts of government and making the efforts of government more difficult by erecting illegal structures everywhere to diminish progress already made and turn very good environment to squalor, something the white people would never do.

These black people are creating poor environmental sanitation whenever government makes effort to make their environment look posh and fit for human habitation. All these are frustrating the efforts of government.

In many cases, people provided with decent RDP houses, either sell or rent out these houses and erect more illegal structures to dwell in with hope of getting more RDP houses from government through fraudulent means and practices whereby killing the good intentions of the housing programs.

Some people who have already benefited from the housing program of government go to different provinces and different counties to live temporarily or permanently and erect illegal structures from place to place. Those with good wages who are entitled to purchase houses with mortgage bonds prefers to live in shacks and pay nothing and wait for RDP housing making the work of government more difficult and creating more shacks than the houses government is building to address the imbalances in society; something the white people cannot do in South Africa. These are some of the problems that are very worrisome and degrading as Africans.

This is why the culture of illegal structures has become a permanent common feature in South Africa, making the world think that the imbalance of the past is not being adequately addressed, or efforts are slow. Worse still those who have benefited from RDP houses in the villages such as in the Eastern Cape move to Cape Town to desecrate the beauty of that mother city with shacks and render urban planning and development a pain in the ass of developers and government.

The attitude of people must change for good in other to see the white clouds in their lives. Government is run by people, and every South African need to work with the people in government to make a great difference that brings hopes and dreams to all South Africans, and to all mankind. As a world, the leaders on earth and the UN as a body have no better work to do than the moral responsibility of ensuring fundamental human rights to basic human needs in life.

Our main focus on earth should be how to provide for each other, and the global economy should be reformed, redressed and addressed to create a better life for all irrespective of our religions, race, or wherever any nation is situated on earth. In this way, the issues of global recessions, climate change, wars and rebellions, and tyranny among nations and leaders of the world will become a non issue.

Leadership is about humanity and not about weapons of human destruction. It is not about how much investments or wealth we create on earth, but how much we have done as humans to make life meaningful and eventful for people on earth. The resources of the earth were not created for us by God for self destruction, but to better the cause of the human race.

Basic human needs are quite different from the needs we seek in other planets. We do not need to waste the resources of the people on earth in space programs and missions because all we need in life is right here on earth. Apollo from the moon cannot cure cancer or diabetes, and it cannot provide food on the table for the children of Iran and North Korea.

We do not need rock samples from mars or signs of water in other planets to water our plants right here on earth to feed our people. While we throw away food in some parts of Europe and other continents around the world, some other people in other places and children are dying daily from hunger and starvation simply because man has not evolved to cater for the needs of others.

We must learn as human beings and as world leaders that earth is the place provided for us by God for human existence, and that weapons of human destructions were not part of God's plans in the creation of natural resources for the people of the world. How we use these resources for mankind is the resultant effect of the kind of life we all face today right here on earth.

We must learn from history that the way we lead the world as leaders is the sad history we read today in world history. We need to re-write the pages of world history by our acts and deeds on earth today.

Re-writing this history can begin by the work of the UN to create a compulsory program of action in ensuring all human beings have roofs over their heads, enough food to eat and to feed their families, proper clothing and provision of Medicare for all on earth. Once this is achieved by all the governments on earth, it will change us into a new world order that will affect positively all the problems we face on earth in every nation.

I believe no one will be interested in acts of violence once there is no hunger on earth, and that people with better life do not destroy the better lives of others. The cause and source of all our troubles and conflicts or the misuse of natural resources is due to lack of basic human needs and human rights in the lives of people. These are the causes of crime and violence in society. Birds have nests; rabbits have holes, and every human being deserve a decent roof over the head. We have but only one earth in one world.

Whether or not our lack of the spirit of togetherness and love have eluded us as a people, one thing is very clear. There is nothing like the first world, second world or third world. There is only one world for all the people on earth. We are all alike in every way and by any means, and no one on earth has crude oil flowing in the veins.

There is nothing like first, second or third world blood flowing in any human veins. There is nothing like white or Caucasian blood, or black and green blood. Blood is red and blood is blood. We all go to the toilet after eating food. No one is eating rocks from mars and drinking Apollo from the moon.

We are all one and the same people on earth with same human wants and needs for human existence in the face of the earth. What we do here on earth today is the legacy and future our generation will inherit from our acts and deeds.

Let us all learn from the legacies left behind by the greatest leader of our time, Nelson Mandela and follow his good examples and footsteps in the Acts of the Apostles for a better new world order. "Together We Can Make a Better Tomorrow!" The time is now!

The End.

To God Be the Glory.

Joe Odiboh